Loyal Soldier

WHILE FIGHTING IN VIETNAM, CAPTAIN HANK (ZVI) WEBB BEGAN SERVING HIS TRUE COMMANDER-IN-CHIEF

As told to
SHAINDY PERL
Author of the bestselling "Tell The World"

ISRAEL BOOKSHOP
LAKEWOOD, NJ

WHILE FIGHTING IN VIETNAM, CAPTAIN HANK (ZVI) WEBB BEGAN SERVING HIS TRUE COMMANDER-IN-CHIEF

As told to
SHAINDY PERL
Author of the bestselling "Tell The World"

Copyright © 2006 by Shaindy Perl

ISBN 1-931681-87-2

All rights reserved. No part of this book may be reproduced or transmitted in any form or by any means (electronic, photocopying, recording or otherwise) without prior written permission of the copyright holder or the distributor.

Cover and book design/Y. Perl
Tel: 845.371.2222 ext. 106

Distributed by:
ISRAEL BOOK SHOP
501 Prospect Street
Lakewood, NJ 08701

Tel: 732.901.3009 ■ 888.536.7427
Fax: 732.901.4012

www.israelbookshop.com

Printed and Bound by:
EASTERN ■ BOOK ■ PRESS ■ INC.
Monsey, NY 10952 ■ 845.352.5600

Printed in Israel

DEDICATION

This book is dedicated to my parents, to whom I owe my very life: my dear father, Yosef ben Shmuel, *o"h* (J. Chester Webb, Esq.), and my dear mother, להבחל״ח Dr. Gertrude M. Webb, *sh'tichye*, of Waltham and Lincoln, MA. Your combined example of living family values has always been a major source of strength and encouragement to me. Your "You can do it if you try" approach to life was, and is, no doubt, responsible for much of what your children may have accomplished so far.

I also dedicate this book to my dear wife, Chaya, *sh'tichye*, and our wonderful children and their families, who give us constant *nachas*: Rabbi "Loozy" and Rochel Fisch of Los Angeles, CA; Rabbi Eitan and Gitty Webb of Princeton, NJ; Rabbi Asher and Doba Webb of Crown Heights, NY; Rabbi Sender and Chami Engel of Long Beach, CA; and our youngest son, Avi Webb of Monsey, NY. All of you volunteered and have been chosen to be active emissaries of the Lubavitcher Rebbe. I consider you all front line soldiers in the army of G-d. May you all continue from strength to strength in all worthwhile endeavors, the most important of which is to bring Moshiach now and make this world a welcome dwelling place for G-d.

TABLE OF CONTENTS

Acknowledgements 8

Prologue 10

- Chapter 1:
  Lone Traveler 13

- Chapter 2:
  My Contract With The Army 35

- Chapter 3:
  Petitioning The Pentagon 47

- Chapter 4:
  Shabbos By Force 65

- Chapter 5:
  Entering The War Zone 85

- Chapter 6:
  Excitement At Quang Tri 103

- Chapter 7:
  Never A Dull Moment 135

- Chapter 8:
  No Welcome Home 147

- Chapter 9:
  The Army Reserves 161

- Chapter 10:
  A New Life 175

- Epilogue:
  A True Soldier Now 189

- Appendix I:
  The Vietnam War 199

- Appendix II:
  U.S. Army Ranks 207

  Glossary 211

Acknowledgements

First and foremost, I must acknowledge G-d's constant Guiding Hand in all that has transpired, and all that continues to happen to me. *Hashgachah pratis*, or individual Divine Providence, while not always apparent at the time it happens, is certainly obvious now to any thinking person. Thank you, Hashem, for leading me in Your ways and for allowing me to grow and try to serve You better in every way, every day.

This book has been in my head for probably thirty years or so. My wife and kids have been urging me to write it for most of that time. Although I attempted to do so many times, distractions, procrastination, etc., etc., prevented the final product from seeing daylight. About one year ago, my friend Rabbi Shmuel Chaim Brunner, whom I meet frequently in the Bobover *shul* in Monsey, NY, and who had heard my story, mentioned that he knew someone who had recently published a bestseller and was interested in my story. Would it be okay if he had her call me?

I agreed, and Mrs. Shaindy Perl contacted me shortly thereafter. She wanted to hear a little bit of my story, so I shared one or two incidents. She was excited about writing about my experiences, and it is to Mrs. Perl that we all owe a debt of gratitude for keeping me on course and seeing the project to the finish.

Her husband, Sruly Perl, gets a big thank you as well, not only for his initial and ongoing enthusiasm and encouragement, but also for nudging me (always with a smile) when I slacked off on meeting deadlines and for his expertise with photography and graphics.

I also want to thank my sister Devorah (Debby) Eisenbach, who saved the many letters I had sent her for so many years. They were an invaluable source of information and many of them appear in the following pages.

The underlying purpose of this book is to move you, the reader, closer to G-d and to inspire you to actualize your own potential to perfect this world and bring Moshiach, for whom the world has been waiting for some 2000 years.

Please note: The names of some people have been changed to protect their privacy. I have tried to be as accurate and truthful as possible, but inadvertent mistakes may have occurred. I take full responsibility for any such errors and/or omissions.

Prologue

"Ah, Captain Webb," Captain Charlie Jones says with exaggerated courtesy, "what brings you here tonight?" He throws his head back and chortles wickedly, knowing that his very presence is disconcerting to me.

I am filled with loathing for this evil, Jew-hating redneck. This surprises me, since when he is around, fear is usually the single dominant emotion I am aware of. After all, this twisted, violent man not only took great pleasure in filling my days with misery, but he actually attempted to murder me in front of some fellow soldiers on one occasion.

As the years of torment flash before my eyes, I see him swaggering into the Officer's Club in Vietnam.

"Webb, I wouldn't even let you into my state, you - - - Jew!" he cries.

He reaches for his weapon, and I instinctively draw back my right hand, make a fist, and land a powerful punch on the nose of my archenemy. I wait for him to stagger backwards, or at least let out a yelp, but nothing happens. Instead, I am suddenly jolted awake by terrible pain. Blood gushes down the side of my face from a deep gash on my forehead. I am completely disoriented, and it takes several moments for me to realize that I am not in Vietnam and Captain Jones is nowhere nearby. In fact, it's been thirty-five years since I've seen him. I hadn't attacked my nemesis after all, but

I did manage to seriously injure myself as I fell against the corner of the night-table in my bedroom.

The commotion has awakened my wife, Chaya. She bolts out of bed, turns on the night lamp and then gapes at me in horror. "Oh my! Zvi! Are you okay?" she gasps.

By now, there's blood all over the place: on my pajama shirt, on the bed, and on the floor. Although I am badly shaken up, I try to keep my voice steady. "I'm all right," I say. "Just another one of those nightmares. I'm afraid I might need some stitches, though."

As my wife drives me through the darkened streets of Monsey toward Good Samaritan Hospital, I can't help feeling a bit annoyed. I haven't seen Captain Jones for years, yet he has somehow managed to hurt me once again, albeit indirectly, in the safety of my own home.

Sitting in the Emergency Room, I reflect on the night's events. I am still haunted by my traumatic experiences in Vietnam, where I had to defend myself not only from enemy soldiers on the battlefield, but at times from those fighting on my side, too. I know that images of those years will stay with me for the rest of my life. However, as I glance at my wife, who is filling out some forms beside me, I take comfort in the fact that at least this is one nightmare that, boruch Hashem, has a truly happy ending. Not only did I eventually leave that war-torn place with my life intact, but in the subsequent years Hashem blessed me with a devoted wife and wonderful children, and I merited to establish a bayis neeman b'Yisrael.

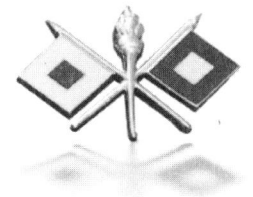

CHAPTER ONE

Lone Traveler

I clutched the carry-on bag that was sitting on my lap and anxiously surveyed my surroundings. The small piece of luggage contained little more than basic necessities. A few changes of clothing and some personal items were packed into another suitcase that was stored in the baggage compartment. After all, a person doesn't need much on a journey like the one I was taking.

Unlike the other passengers on the plane, who, I assumed, already knew how they would spend their time in South America, I had no specific destination in mind. I hoped to visit my sister Sally, who was serving with the Peace Corps, but otherwise, I hadn't made any plans. I had purchased my ticket with a single goal in mind: I was going to spend time away from everyone and simply think, explore, and try to find myself. A trunk full of belongings, I believed, would hinder, rather than help, my search.

During the past few years, I had been battling endlessly with tumultuous emotions, trying unsuccessfully to find inner peace and contentment. I was wrestling with my identity and began questioning my choice of profession.

I had graduated with a bachelor's degree in journalism from Boston University in 1964, and after spending the summer working in public relations for Chrysler Corporation in Detroit, Michigan, I began studying law at Suffolk University in Boston, Massachusetts. During my first year there, I won the school's "moot court" competition by arguing a complicated contract case. Despite my victory, I flunked the end of year contracts exam by only a fraction of a point and had to repeat the grade. It was a frustrating experience, and the next two years were filled with unrest and self-doubt.

In addition to the disappointment of narrowly missing the grade, I was having qualms about my choice of profession. Why was I going to law school anyway, I wondered. Was it because I wanted to be a lawyer, or was I merely trying to please my father when my true calling lay elsewhere?

At Boston University I had greatly enjoyed my classes on journalism, and my professor, David Manning White, was very satisfied with my work. "Webb," he told me one day, "you don't have to continue coming to class if you don't want to. You will receive a straight A regardless."

I seriously began to consider pursuing a career in journalism at the time. I felt that I could accomplish more for society by speaking out with my pen than by spending countless hours in a courtroom engaging in lengthy debates that lasted for months. Moreover, it was work that I truly *enjoyed*. Still, after much persuasion by my father, I had enrolled in law school, a decision I now came to regret. While I had certainly gained valuable knowledge and skills, I didn't find much appeal in the long, drawn out orations and arguments that are such a vital part of the profession. So why was I wasting my time studying to be a lawyer?

I was in a state of confusion, and I desperately needed to escape from everything, clear my head, and think in peace. In short, I needed to figure out what to do with my life.

Thus, in early February of 1968, I purchased a plane ticket to South America. Now, as I sat on the plane, I trembled with excitement and anticipation. Although I had done more than my share of traveling during the 26 years of my life, this was the first time that I was taking such a major trip alone. Hoping to find inspiration in some of the different countries' beautiful and exotic locations, I headed towards a journey of adventure and introspection.

• • •

I was born on May 11, 1942, the oldest child of my parents Joseph Chester Webb and Gertrude Mikels Webb. Named Harrison Eli at birth, I soon became known to everyone as Hank. My siblings, Sally, Marc, Debby, Sam, and Heidi, followed in quick succession. Sadly, the seventh child, Joshua, died in infancy.

My father, who was born in the summer of 1914, was known to family and friends as Chet. A successful, hardworking lawyer, he was a man of great integrity, valuing honesty above all else. He was a strong, principled person who was very passionate about his beliefs. Dad was also gregarious by nature, very social and outgoing and ready to strike up a conversation with anyone.

My mother, Gertrude, was born in July 1916. She nurtured her brood with love and was very devoted to her children. She always took the time to listen to our stories and empathize with us.

In addition to caring for her family, Mom was a dedicated teacher. She earned a doctorate in education and became very active in assisting children with learning disabilities, particularly those with dyslexia. She gave lectures and wrote articles to help educators understand their plight and learn how to teach and deal with dyslexic children. She eventually developed a program for language-disabled students called PAL, the Program for Advancement of Learning, and later also founded the Webb International Center for Dyslexia, or WICD, the latter of which she is still involved with today.

Although my parents were both born in the United States, they were raised in very different environments.

My paternal grandfather, Samuel Lubawitz, had come to the United States from Lithuania in the early 1900's as a young man. Initially, he stayed at the home of an uncle, Gershon Lubawitz Werbolsky, who had changed his name to Gerald Webb, and Samuel soon adopted the name Webb for himself, as well.

Grandpa Webb was very ambitious. Upon arriving in the United States, he immediately enrolled in and then completed Waltham's Business School, while supporting himself by taking a job at Hood's Milk Company. Afterwards, he trained in a Boston lawyer's office and in four years passed the Massachusetts Bar to open his own law firm.

His father, Rav Eliezer Lubawitz, was a well-learned Jew, who had raised Grandpa Webb with a Torah education. In America, Grandpa Webb continued his Talmudic studies by joining "Chevra Shas" in Boston. Like most of the other members, the observant aspect of his Judaism fell by the wayside, while the intellectual interest remained.

Samuel married my grandmother, Goldie Rochel Pearlstein, on June 17, 1913. Unlike Samuel, who had immigrated in his youth, Goldie was born and raised in America. She was the daughter of a prominent family, and the marriage further secured Samuel's position in Boston's elite Jewish society.

Thus, my father was born into an illustrious Boston family that tried very hard to assimilate into the fold of American society. They belonged to Temple Israel, a Reform congregation that considered itself an enlightened and sophisticated community. Most of the members were well-established, wealthy professionals, who were proud of their liberal and modern viewpoints and lifestyles.

When my father was a teenager, life suddenly took an unexpected turn. Grandpa Samuel Webb became ill with a degenerative disease. His condition worsened slowly but steadily, and soon he was no longer able to work at his law office. As their savings dwindled to nothing, the family fell on hard times.

As the oldest son, my father was forced to begin working to support his family. To his distress, the well-to-do cousins and friends who had once been his buddies began giving him the cold shoulder. Then, after the family moved out of their spacious apartment in the upper class Boston neighborhood, these friends considered it beneath their dignity to be associated with him anymore.

While my father was troubled by these difficult developments, they were destined to lead him to his future wife, who grew up "on the other side of the railroad tracks." My mother's parents, Arthur and Ida Mikels, had both come from Russia to America with their families in the late 1800's. They were married in 1910 and lived in the blue-collar section of town. Grandpa Mikels supported his family with a small store, Arthur's Flower Shop.

My mother was my grandparents' third child, preceded by a daughter, Edith, and a son, Leo. Although she was named Goldie at birth, her name was changed to Gertrude by her first grade teacher.

The Mikels were less assimilated and led a much more traditional life. Grandpa Arthur Mikels put on *tefillin* every morning before breakfast. In addition, they kept kosher and observed many of the Jewish customs they had witnessed in their parents' homes. In fact, years later, my mother also had some very strict "rules" in her own home; for example, we children were forbidden to taste *matzah* on Erev Pesach. Only much later did I learn that many such practices were actually based on *halachah*.

When my father met the Mikels family, it was clear that they lacked some of the sophistication he was accustomed to from his youth. However, after his early life experiences, that stylish, upper class aloofness no longer held the same appeal it once did, and he was more attracted to the Mikels' warmth and sincerity.

My parents were married on June 29, 1941, and moved to the Boston suburb of Waltham, Massachusetts, where I was born. A blue-collar town with hard-working, friendly people, they deemed it the perfect place to raise their growing family. Initially, our family lived in a house on South Street, but in 1950, my parents bought a beautiful piece of land on the bank of the Charles River and built our family home there.

Although the Jews in Waltham were greatly outnumbered by Christians, the town did have a small Conserva-dox congregation, which my parents joined. The rabbi, Rabbi Aaron Kra, was an Orthodox man, but religion played only a minor role in the everyday lives of most of his congregants.

My parents had received only a minimal Jewish education, but they were both very proud of their Jewish heritage. They kept an assortment of traditions and celebrated the *yomim tovim* to the best of their ability. On Rosh Hoshana and Yom Kippur the entire family attended services in *shul*; on Chanukah we lit some colorful candles; and on Pesach, we all took part in a *seder* together with a number of invited guests—not all of whom were Jewish—and took turns reading some pages out of a Maxwell House Haggada. (Once, I remember, we were invited to do a mock *seder* in a church. It was an interesting experience, but I sensed something wasn't "*kosher*" about it.)

For a period of time, my siblings and I were enrolled in a Jewish after-school program, which held classes for Jewish children several afternoons each week. We learned the *aleph beis*, read about the *parshah*, and studied some Jewish history. The classes were not difficult at all, and they were taught in a leisurely, informal environment.

While the teacher, Mr. Weiner, was able to educate us about our Jewish heritage, there was no one to turn to with questions of content. If a child asked a question that the teacher could not answer, the response was always the same: "That's the way we do things."

Despite their limited knowledge of Jewish law and history, my parents did have a very strong sense of Jewish identity, which they tried to pass on to us. In fact, one of my earliest memories involves an incident that demonstrates this point.

I was attending kindergarten in the local public school, when, one day at home, my mother overheard me singing a Christian song that I had learned in school. As soon as she realized what the words were, she dropped what she was doing and rushed to my side.

"Hank, what are you singing?" she asked, horrified.

I was bewildered by her sudden excitement and tried to figure out what I had done wrong. "It's the song we sing in school, Mom," I replied. "Don't you like it?"

Cupping my chin, my mother looked into my eyes. "I don't ever want to hear you singing that song again. Do you understand?"

Although I was taken aback by her reaction to the song and couldn't imagine why it had upset her so, her solemn tone told me that this was not the right time for questions. "Okay, I won't sing it again," I promised.

The very next day, Mom marched down to school with me, clutching my hand tightly. She accompanied me all the way into the classroom and strode purposefully toward my teacher.

"I overhead Hank singing 'J. Loves Me' while playing with his toys at home yesterday," she said. "Why are you teaching religious songs to kids in public school?"

"I'm sorry, but it's part of my curriculum," the teacher responded. "I like to sing it with the children. It gives them a sense of security."

"But we're Jewish," my mother insisted. "I don't want Hank singing any Christian songs."

"No problem," the teacher said. "I'll make sure that Hank doesn't join in when we sing that song in the future."

With a sigh of relief, Mom thanked the teacher and kissed me good-bye. Later in the day, my teacher announced to the class that Hank Webb would not be required to sing "J. Loves Me" with everyone else.

Her announcement made me feel very uncomfortable, and I wondered why I was being singled out. Although I didn't understand all that was going on, the incident left me with a profound lesson: being Jewish meant that I was different. There was "them" and there was "us" and some invisible line would always separate the two.

Every now and then there would be another event that emphasized this point. When I was in the sixth grade, for example, I visited the house of a close friend whose family was somewhat Evangelical. During my visit, the issue of religion came up. My friend and his mother, both passionate believers, tried to persuade me of the importance of getting "saved" and accepting J. as my savior. "Otherwise you will burn in hell forever," they warned.

They were good people who meant well. While I knew that their beliefs directly contradicted the Jewish viewpoint, I was unable to defend my own religion. My limited knowledge did not provide me with even one argument, and all I could say was, "Oh, we don't believe in all that."

When I repeated the conversation to my parents that night, they were incensed. "I forbid you to step into that house again," my father thundered.

Ironically, in junior high school, it was a Christian student who made sure I wouldn't forget my heritage. A big bully named Steve Samborski used to pick on me regularly because I was Jewish. Once he beat me up in the school playground, and an Italian friend (I think it was Steve Graceffa) and some others came to my defense and rescued me.

Years later, one of my sisters began dating a non-Jewish boy. To my father's chagrin, the relationship soon turned serious, despite his explicit disapproval of it. One day, in a fit of rage, he physically threw the unsuspecting visitor out of our house.

Again, I was taken aback by this incredible passion for the sake of religion. After all, my father prided himself in being a liberal, open-minded thinker. He believed in the equality of all races and was even prepared to defend the rights of a criminal in a court of law—regardless of color or creed. And yet, when the Jewish identity of a member of his family was being threatened, those "equals" suddenly became "outsiders."

For me, it was difficult to evoke the same Jewish fervor. Religion, after all, played such a minor role in my life. Why, then, should I worry about singing a Christian song or dating a non-Jewish girl?

One "Jewish experience" that does stand out in my mind is the year that I accompanied my father to *shul* every morning, where he put on *tefillin* and said *Kaddish* for his father, Grandpa Webb. I was nine at the time, and these daily excursions gave me a very real and constant connection to my heritage. During the prayers, I would go around with a little box collecting charity from the congregants.

After my baby brother Joshua died in February 1960, I also felt somewhat of a spiritual awakening. I was especially touched by my parents' strong faith in Hashem and their acceptance of His decision to take their little baby boy.

Indeed, not only did my parents have a deep trust in Hashem, but they also had a very strong sense of morality. They expected us to conduct ourselves properly, show respect for our siblings, and honor our parents. My father treated my mother with exceptional consideration and insisted that we do the same. He also continuously preached about the importance of integrity and truthfulness. "There's no such thing as being very honest," he often declared. "Either you're honest or dishonest."

Impressed by my parents' repeated admonitions that "your siblings are your best friends," we children got along exceptionally well. We were a very close-knit family and we had the good fortune to enjoy a very wonderful, carefree childhood.

One of things that my family took a special interest in was music. I eventually learned to play the piano, organ, bass fiddle, and guitar. My sister Heidi played moving melodies on her flute, and others in the family were proficient as well.

The happiest memories that I share with my siblings to this day, though, are those of the adventurous road trips our family embarked on each year. Every summer, my father would take some time off from his successful law practice, and for about six to eight weeks, a small tent became our home. Later, a camping trailer was custom built for our family and hitched to the back of our station wagon. The double beds that dropped out of the walls became our sleeping quarters, and we ate the meals that my mother cooked in the trailer's tiny kitchenette.

We traveled for days on end, covering several hundred miles at one time. We stopped every so often to enjoy breathtaking scenic landscapes and hike through overgrown forest trails. At times, we left the trailer in a trailer park for several hours and spent the day touring various museums and historic sites in nearby cities.

Over the years, we passed through almost every one of the fifty states, even reaching as far as Alaska one summer. My parents believed that these cross-country journeys were an educational experience, and we did indeed learn much from them. We met a number of interesting people and visited places that many only read about. Sometimes we stopped to find the local synagogue and meet the Jews in that area. During the course of our travels, we visited synagogues in the most unusual locations, such as Mexico, Alaska, and Guatemala.

Our trips were filled with many unforgettable moments that I enjoy reminiscing about even today. One summer, for instance, my father "invented" a washing machine. He took a large ash barrel and filled it with soapy water. He deposited the dirty laundry into the bucket, where it agitated as the car traveled. After about one hundred miles, the bucket was emptied and clean water from a gas station was hosed in. After another one hundred miles, the clothes had been washed and rinsed, and we strung them across the trailer to dry.

Of course, there were also some unpleasant experiences. During one of our trips, we visited New Orleans. We were traveling with two cars that year, and one of them was giving us trouble. After we pulled into the campsite on the outskirts of the city, Dad left to take the car to a shop.

It was a very hot day, and my siblings and I were eager to go for a swim in Lake Pontchartrain to cool off. We piled into the car and my mother drove us to the nearest beach. When we got there, we learned that the fee was $1 per person. Of course, the value of a dollar was much more back then, and since there were five people in our party, Mom, myself, Sal, Marc, and Debby, the total amounted to a pretty sum. "All that money just to dunk our feet in water!" my mother exclaimed. "That seems excessive for a quick dip in the lake."

We followed her dejectedly back to our car, beads of sweat running down our long faces. "Don't worry," Mom reassured us when we were seated again. "We'll continue down the road, and I'm sure we'll find a cheaper place elsewhere."

We continued on the same road and stopped again several minutes later when we spotted a path that led down to the lake. We eagerly jumped out and scampered towards the water.

"Hey, where do you think you're going?" a heavyset man yelled excitedly, waving his hands to get our attention.

We stopped in surprise, staring at his angry, agitated face. "We're just going for a quick swim," my mother explained.

"No you're not," he said. "This part of the lake is for colored people. Only blacks are allowed here. Get out!"

I opened my mouth to protest, eager to debate the issue with him. My mother quickly glanced at me and knew immediately what I wanted to do. "Quiet! Don't say a word!" she hissed nervously. Yanking me by the arm, she pushed me towards the car.

We hurried back to our vehicle. As we pulled away, we realized that the man was right behind us. He followed us until we were almost back at our campsite, wanting to make sure that we meddlesome Northerners wouldn't corrupt the area by breaking the strict, sacred laws of segregation.

We were all anxious and on edge as we finally pulled into the campsite. That man was the first redneck we had ever seen, and surprisingly, he really did have a thick, red neck and an angry face. His fury had frightened us, and we were all subdued as we got out of the car.

Several days earlier, we had been surprised to see a lavatory marked "Colored" when we stopped to use the public restrooms. Now, we had gotten firsthand experience of the hatred and prejudice that festered in the area. As soon as my father returned from the shop, my mother said to him, "Let's get out of here. New Orleans may be a beautiful city, but this place is giving me the creeps. I want to leave immediately."

On another occasion, when we were at a campsite in Georgia, I struck up a conversation with some people and the subject soon turned to civil rights, an intensely-debated issue at the time. Earlier that day, we had been disturbed to see black people riding in the back of buses, and I was interested to hear more about their living conditions.

"These people are different," the other campers explained. "The two races are not supposed to mingle. We must lead separate lives and have laws that help us keep our distance from each other."

Before long, we discovered that these weren't the only people the Georgians despised. During the course of our conversation, one of us mentioned that we were Jewish, and their attitude toward our family changed drastically. They suddenly became cold and hostile, and we could sense their hateful stares even when our backs were turned.

"You had better get out of here," one of them told my father threateningly. "You don't share our ideas, and we don't need you dirty Jews polluting our neighborhoods. If you know what's good for you, you won't keep your family here a moment longer."

It wasn't the first time I experienced such open anti-Semitism, but still I could not understand what made them loathe us so. It soon became clear, though, that these were no empty threats, and the people there would not hesitate to harm us.

My father was not one to run from confrontation, but he now realized that his family's safety was in jeopardy. It was the first time that I had seen him in such palpable fear. Even though it was already late at night, he ordered us to pack our belongings quickly. We hurriedly left the campsite and were soon on the road again.

On another occasion, we were driving up a very steep mountain when the car's engine gave out. It had been hauling the heavy trailer up the mountain road, and the weight was obviously more than it could handle. All of a sudden, the car stalled and started rolling backwards. My father pressed the trailer's air brakes, but the car continued sliding down.

"Quick! Everyone get out! Get out of the car!" my father ordered.

Only after we were all out did my father jump out, and not a moment too soon. With the trailer in tow, the car continued rolling backwards until it fell off the mountain. The family gaped in horror as the trailer crashed down the mountainside for a distance of twenty to thirty feet, where it got caught in some trees.

"Don't worry," my father said, trying to calm us. "It's only money. Everyone's okay; nobody got hurt. That's what matters."

At that moment, I felt a new respect for my father. I admired the fact that he had waited until we were all out of the vehicle before jumping for safety himself, and I was impressed to see that he had kept his head throughout, managing to control his underlying panic. It had been a frightening experience for all of us, and he had proven himself to be a reliable protector of his family.

These unforgettable moments on our trips, both good and bad, bonded the family like nothing else could. We talked about the trip for weeks after our return home, and before the last piece of luggage was unpacked, we were already planning the next year's adventure.

Thus, it is no wonder that when I reached a crisis in my personal life, I reacted by purchasing a plane ticket. I had simply looked back at the happiest memories of my youth and concluded that the best way to solve my problems was to hit the road again.

• • •

Just before I embarked on my trip to South America, my sister Debby and I had a long talk. Debby, who is seven years my junior, was the most spiritual-minded of the family, and the two of us had always gotten along exceptionally well. She knew that I was going through some tough times and wanted to support and reassure me. "You know, Hank," she said, "if you ever feel lost, just go into the nearest synagogue and you'll be home."

She said it with such sincerity and simplicity that her words went straight into my heart.

The first country I visited in South America was Brazil. I spent some time in the city of Belém, where I met a non-Jewish girl who wanted to improve her English and was willing to teach me some Portuguese. On Friday night, I recalled Debby's words and asked the girl to lead me to the local synagogue. We walked there together, and she waited while I joined the Friday night services.

The next morning I went back to *shul* without her. I already knew my way around on my own, and besides, I sensed that she was not welcomed by the congregants, since she was obviously not Jewish. I was invited by someone to join his family for Shabbos lunch, and I thoroughly enjoyed the experience.

(While speaking to my host, I learned that the congregation desperately needed prayer books, *chumashim*, and other Jewish literature. After returning home, Debby and I packed up a box of *seforim* and shipped it off to them. Later, we received a very warm thank you note from the community.)

While in Belém, I signed up for a boat trip through the Amazon jungle, which lasted for about ten days. It was the most beautiful, awesome sight I had ever seen. The boat took us up the Amazon River, where we saw crocodiles and alligators swimming around in the water. One had to be careful not to fall overboard, since the basin also contains Piranhas, man-eating fish which measure only about eight inches in length. They are armed with strong jaws and razor-sharp, triangular teeth, which allow them to chop off pieces of flesh from a victim with alarming efficiency. And with so many of them swimming together, they can devour large, wounded animals—and sometimes humans—in no time at all.

The rain forests we passed were also a sight to behold. Beautiful, multi-colored birds filled the jungle with the sounds of their melodious chirping. Tall, majestic trees towered over us, and we could see some magnificent rubber trees, which flourish in the area. We were also able to observe the natives in several small villages that we passed. Their living conditions were so primitive, that they appeared to have stepped right off the pages of a history book. Clothing was scanty, and their homes were flimsy huts of straw, as far as I could see. Every now and then, the boat pulled up to shore, and we were able to step off and look around for a little while.

During the cruise, I met a nice, intelligent German girl who was traveling with her parents. My Shabbos experience in Belém had heightened my appreciation for Jews and Judaism, but not to the extent that I wouldn't consider dating a non-Jewish girl. We hit it off right away and began spending much of our time together. I seemed to have made a good impression on her parents, too, since they were very cordial and friendly, asking me about my family and schooling. They seemed to like the fact that my parents were professionals and I had gone to college.

As the four of us were conversing one day, I mentioned that my family was Jewish. To my surprise, my remark caused their attitude towards me to change completely. Their warm smiles disappeared, and they suddenly became cold and aloof. The couple politely told me that I would no longer be able to spend time with their daughter, and the three of them quickly walked away.

I was flabbergasted. "These people are so narrow-minded and bigoted!" I thought. "One minute they think I'm a nice young man and the next minute they don't want to socialize with me because I'm Jewish."

Suddenly, I recalled my father's reaction to the non-Jewish dates that we brought home. Not only do Jewish parents forbid their children to marry out, I realized, but people of other faiths also don't want us to mingle. This experience was a true eye-opener for me, as I learned that not only Jews dislike mixed unions. I had never considered that the parents of my non-Jewish dates might share my own parents' viewpoint.

When the Amazon River tour was complete, I went to São Paulo, where my sister Sally was working with the Peace Corps. There were important health issues to be addressed, since many natives were dying from contaminated drinking water. Sally was helping with water purification and the immunization of the local population. Many of the people lived in abject poverty and could not afford to provide medical care for the ill. For these families, even basic necessities were hard to come by.

From São Paulo, I continued to Uruguay, Peru, and Ecuador. It was fascinating to observe the different cultures. Most of the natives lacked modern day comforts and lived a life of hardship and need. Even simple bus rides were an adventure, as people carried live poultry home from the market and chickens and roosters would be flapping about. Unlike me, the others on the bus took all the squawking and flying around in stride; for them, it was part of the regular bus riding experience.

Finally, after six weeks of living a nomad's life, my wandering came to an end. I returned to the United States with dozens of colorful stories of excitement and adventure. Nonetheless, while I had been rejuvenated and uplifted by my travels, I had to admit that my quest for improved self-awareness had not met with much success. True, the tension and anxiety had disappeared, but discontent continued to churn just beneath the surface. I had come no closer to finding the inner peace I yearned for.

By now, my turbulent emotions were driving me insane. I had still not made a decision about my future and was reluctant to resume my studies in law school. Thus, in desperation, I decided to put my life on hold.

"This time, though," I thought determinedly, "I won't merely run off for a few short weeks. Instead, I will take a *real* break. I will go someplace far away from school, family, and friends and stay there long enough so that I can figure out what I want to do with my life."

But where could I possibly escape to?

Fortunately, it didn't take long to figure out the solution to my problems. I already had a previous obligation, and there was no better time to fulfill it. In doing so, I would be provided with food and shelter and kept isolated from the rest of society for an extended period. Moreover, I thought with a smile, my decision to leave would actually be applauded.

MacArthur Great Words

Prayer for His Son Eloquent Piety

WASHINGTON (AP) — Gen Douglas MacArthur is leaving a spiritual legacy to his son, Arthur—a father's prayer he wrote in the Philippines during the desperate early days of the Pacific war.

According to the general's biographer and confidant, Maj Gen Courtney Whitney, the family repeated this MacArthur credo many times during early morning devotions:

"Build me a son, O Lord, who will be strong enough to know when he is weak, and brave enough to face himself when he is afraid; one who will be proud and unbending in honest defeat, and humble and gentle in victory.

"Build me a son whose wishes will not take the place of deeds; a son who will know Thee—and that to know himself is the foundation stone of knowledge.

"Lead him, I pray, not in the path of ease and comfort, but under the stress and spur of difficulties and challenge. Here let him learn to stand up in the storm; here let him learn compassion for those who fail.

"Build me a son whose heart will be clear, whose goal will be high, a son who will master himself before he seeks to master other men, one who will reach into the future, yet never forget the past.

"And after all these things are his, add, I pray, enough of a sense of humor, so that he may always be serious, yet never take himself too seriously. Give him humility, so that he may always remember the simplicity of true greatness, the open mind of true wisdom, and the meekness of true strength.

"Then I, his father, will dare to whisper, 'I have not lived in vain.'"

This newspaper clipping hung on the wall of my father's office. I frequently read it during visits to his workplace, and it made a great impression on me.

CHAPTER TWO

MY CONTRACT WITH THE ARMY

The Reserve Officer Training Corps (ROTC) is a program run by the United States Army at over 250 colleges and universities around the country. The ROTC recruits students, who agree to attend a course known as "Military Science" in addition to the other classes they take. There, students study the history of the army, names and functions of various weapons, military protocols, and the procedures for writing official reports, earning college credits as they would for any other course. In addition to the classes, students also receive military uniforms and attend parade drills to learn how to march in official ceremonies. Then, when graduating from college, the students are commissioned to the rank of Second Lieutenant and are required to serve two years of active duty as an officer in the United States Army, as well as two more years in the Army Reserves.

Boston University is also affiliated with the ROTC. During my years as an undergraduate student there, I decided to sign up for the program. There were several factors that prompted this decision.

First of all, although the country hadn't yet been hit by the anti-war riots and demonstrations that would soon wreak havoc across the nation, there were already American troops stationed in Vietnam at this time. As a Jew, I had been taught to value the individual's rights and liberties as protected by the Constitution. In law school, I gained an even deeper appreciation of constitutional rights, and I was eager to make a commitment to support these values and spread democracy to other areas of the world. I was hoping to join the soldiers in Vietnam once my studies were completed and help shield the South Vietnamese people from the yoke of Communism. It was my understanding that the South Vietnamese government had requested that the United States help defend them against communist aggression and that the South Vietnamese people really wanted to live in peaceful democracy.

Secondly, I was raised in a very patriotic environment, and national pride was instilled in me since my early youth. In fact, my great uncle Julius Seltzer, who married Grandma Mikels' sister Rebecca, was the first Jew to live in the historical town of Lexington. He moved there with his wife in 1902 and owned a tailor shop opposite the statue of the Minuteman. Descendants of the original Minutemen would bring their uniforms for mending or summer storage, and Uncle Julius became intrigued by the stories they told. He began sharing them with tourists who visited the area, and eventually he became captain of the

Republican Minutemen's society. He was also instrumental in instituting the annual April 19th parade to commemorate the first skirmish of the American Revolution that took place there in 1775. Indeed, I distinctly recall visiting Lexington with some of my siblings as a little boy and being enthused by Uncle Julius' dramatic account of the Minutemen's bravery.

Moreover, several members of my family, including my father, had served in the military. In fact, my father's brother, Stanley Webb, took part in the Normandy invasion during World War II and eventually reached the rank of colonel. The military had played an important role in their lives, and they encouraged me to join the ROTC.

Finally, I realized that there was a good chance that I would eventually be drafted into the U.S. Military. If that were to happen, I would be starting out at the very bottom of the military hierarchy, as an enlisted soldier. By joining the ROTC, I would be able to bypass all the enlisted ranks and hold the rank of Lieutenant right away. Being an officer meant that I would be in a leadership position when I served and that I would be spared the menial and more tedious work that is generally assigned to enlisted personnel. In addition, I would be paid better than non-commissioned soldiers once I began active duty.

Thus, I soon found myself in a classroom on campus listening to the lectures of an army officer. Occasionally, the class was taken to firing ranges nearby for target practice, but most of the material was taught in a regular classroom environment. When practicing parade drills, we proudly marched across the campus in our army uniforms, holding our heads a little higher, and our backs a bit straighter than usual.

When I graduated from Boston University in June of 1964, I officially became a Second Lieutenant, which is the lowest officer rank. I was able to obtain a deferment from active duty in order to attend law school. While studying law, I was automatically promoted to the rank of First Lieutenant.

In reality, since I had obtained a deferment, I was able to delay my active duty service until I graduated from law school. Nonetheless, as I was going through a difficult period in my life, I decided to leave school temporarily. Since I had this two-year obligation to the United States Army, which I would have to fulfill sooner or later anyhow, I figured there was no better time to begin my active service. The army was the ideal adventure, as well as a place to escape. I hoped that by the time I completed my two year commitment, my inner conflicts would be resolved and my plans for the future would be settled.

In retrospect, I realize that it was *hashgachah pratis* that I wasn't doing well in law school. After all, this led me to doubt my choice of profession and begin questioning everything about my life. Thus, I eventually left to join the army, where my life took a new direction.

Soon after I notified the army that I was ready to begin my service, I visited the doctor for the required physical examination. During the visit, the physician questioned me about my twice dislocated left shoulder. I had first injured it during a football game when I was about sixteen years old and played for my high school team. Then, while riding on my motor bike several years later, I hit a pothole and was thrown over the handlebars. Once again, I dislocated the shoulder, and a passing motorist rushed me to the hospital. This time I was warned that if I injured my shoulder again I would require surgery to set it back in place.

"You know," the doctor remarked, "I could exempt you from service on account of that troublesome shoulder. It obviously wouldn't take much for you to hurt it again."

"No, thanks," I replied. "I really do want to fulfill my obligation to Uncle Sam."

I had given my word to the United States Army, and I was determined to honor it. I was not looking for an easy way out.

Shortly thereafter I received my orders in the mail, instructing me to appear at Fort Gordon, Georgia on May 1, 1968, to begin basic training.

Boot camp was a grueling experience. We were up each morning at the crack of dawn and were expected to run several miles before breakfast. In fact, even during the day, we never stopped running. Whenever we had to get from one place to another, we jogged. We ran to the classroom; we ran to the mess hall; and we ran to our sleeping quarters. A leisurely stroll, even when not under the supervision of the drill sergeants, was simply unacceptable.

There was a rigorous PT (physical training) program, and we did numerous push-ups and sit-ups. During the entire day, we were surrounded by tough drill sergeants, who kept bellowing orders. Any misdemeanor was punished with additional strenuous workouts. Although we were all officers in the class, during basic training we were all addressed as "cadets."

Much of the screaming directed at us by the drill sergeants was purely for psychological purposes. During basic training, the army tries to strip soldiers of their personality and individuality and instill the concept of following the orders of a higher authority almost instinctively. One must become a number and follower, a G.I. with no personal opinion. One cannot think for himself or question the commands of a superior.

In truth, this submission to authority is crucial on the battlefield. During wartime, no military operation can be successful if soldiers second-guess each decision made by their leader or offer other opinions. They cannot hesitate about, or deliberate on, each command, but must respond instantly as one. However, this unquestioning faith in higher authority would serve me well later in my personal life when I turned to *Yiddishkeit*. In many ways, an observant lifestyle resembles that of a soldier, only then we are *m'vatel* ourselves and are subordinates of the *true* Commander-in-Chief, *Hakadosh Baruch Hu*.

At Fort Gordon, we learned to dismantle, clean, and quickly reassemble various weapons. Together with the other men, I swung across canyons on ropes and climbed steep cliffs; I scaled walls and crawled under barbed wire fences. I conquered fears I never knew I had and learned skills I hoped I would never use.

One day during basic training, the drill sergeants ordered us into a trailer that had been filled with gas. We were issued gas masks, but were ordered to take them off for a short period once we were inside. The sensation was unlike anything I had ever experienced. My eyes stung and became teary and my stomach felt queasy. It was a very uncomfortable feeling, and a number of men became sick. By the time we stumbled out of there, we had all learned the importance of guarding our protective gear carefully and realized that it could indeed save our lives. As our drill sergeants suspected, no lecture could have brought home that point quite as well.

At Fort Gordon, I also took a course to train for my specialty, which was to be a Signal officer. I learned how to install and repair radios and other communications equipment; the various frequencies used by the military, and for which purpose each one is designated; and the special methods and codes for transferring classified material.

All in all, I was doing very well in Fort Gordon. I passed most of my courses with flying colors and was even awarded a medal. I was proud of my achievements and once more felt good about myself. I was pleased with my decision to begin my active duty.

After the first couple of weeks of basic training, we were occasionally issued passes that allowed us to go off base for a short period. One time, I received such a pass just before Tisha b'Av, and I decided to visit a synagogue in the nearby town.

Upon entering the synagogue, I found a group of people sitting in a circle on the floor, as they took turns reading the story of the *churban* in English. I had never seen such a gathering, and I joined them in mourning the destruction of the second Beis Hamikdash. I also read several paragraphs out loud, experiencing for the first time a sense of communal sadness and loss over the Jewish tragedy of long ago. My Jewish spark was gradually becoming less dormant.

I completed my basic training in July and was transferred to Fort Sill, Oklahoma, where I took an advanced course for Signal officers at the United States Army Artillery and Missile School.

It was a really beautiful place, with golf courses, swimming pools, air-conditioned apartments and several gymnasiums, in addition to the usual firing ranges, classrooms, and airfields.

While I was already familiar with the many different types of signal equipment, I now learned how to identify, through various map coordinates and compass calculations, the exact location of friendly or enemy positions. This is known as "shooting Azimuths." When a soldier is out in the field and calling for help, he doesn't always know his exact location. Artillery support troops must determine the soldier's position. It is crucial that they be very accurate, because when this information is passed on and artillery or air support is dispatched, the pilots and gunners rely on it to avoid hitting their own people and score direct hits on enemy positions.

A considerable amount of time was also spent studying the methods for encrypting messages quickly and efficiently. After all, when reports are sent out, detailing the exact position of the soldiers during battle, this information must be protected to prevent the enemy from using it to their own advantage. Thus, all messages must be encrypted, and so we had to become familiar with the complex procedures used to ensure that reports remain secure.

Curiously, there were four Jordanians in my class in Fort Sill who had come to the United States especially to take this advanced communications course. Although I wondered why the United States Army had agreed to train these foreign soldiers, I had no trouble getting along with them. We drank coffee together, talked about the lessons, and exchanged stories. One day, however, they discovered that I was Jewish and our association came to an abrupt end.

I experienced a sense of déjà vu, as I recalled the anti-Semitic incident in Georgia, the playground beatings in junior high school, and the German family on the Amazon tour. The Jordanians, though, weren't content with merely ignoring me. Hardly a year had passed since the 1967 Six Day War, and they considered every Jew an archenemy. They were openly hostile and tried making my life miserable by telling the American students to stop speaking to me, too. Fortunately, most of the others in the class pretended not to notice the friction between us and refused to take sides and become involved in the conflict.

Fort Sill, however, didn't only provide me with unpleasant experiences. During my time on the base, I learned that I could take a piloting course and the government would pay for ninety percent of the cost. I jumped at this unique opportunity and immediately signed up for afternoon lessons. Our classes ended at 1500 hours (3:00 p.m.), and while the others spent the rest of the day carousing at bars in a nearby town, I learned how to fly small planes. Although the lessons were more challenging than I had first expected, I thoroughly enjoyed the course and looked forward to receiving my pilot's license.

At last, my time in Fort Sill was drawing to an end. I finished the 11-week advanced Signal Corps course in early October 1968. While some of my buddies received orders for deployment to Vietnam, I was instructed to report to Fort Meade, Maryland, for my first official assignment.

UNITED STATES ARMY ARTILLERY AND MISSILE CENTER
FORT SILL, OKLAHOMA

11 August, '68

Dear Debby,

Thanks so much for your prompt and terrific line of recent date. (I say "recent" because my Hebrew is so embarrassingly inadequate that I can't figure out what date you wrote it). Your explorations through Old Jerusalem sound fascinating, and your comment about Arabs being apparently friendly and even selling pictures of Moshe Dayan... While such a situation sounds incongruous to news reports, it just shows further that people as individuals cannot always be expected to behave as their governments, families, religions, or cultures would have them behave. It's obvious that your horizons are being broadened quickly. May you always be able to use your newfound experiences and knowledge to the ultimate degree of "good"-doing. ...

Friday night I went to shul here for the 2nd time. It's at the Brigade Chapel and is the only synagogue for many miles. The city of Lawton does not have one, so the few Jewish families who live in Lawton come to Fort Sill for services. We just about get enough for a minion (sic), but it's a very interesting and meaningful service because of some of the problems some people (especially enlisted men) have to go through to get to services. They show up in dirty fatigues with earplugs dangling from shirt pockets—because they've been out firing guns on some range—but somehow by 8:10 or so they manage to get there. Not quite the same circumstances as in Newton or Waltham, huh? ...

I guess I already told you I'm taking flying lessons. ... Not much other news now. Take care, stay happy and healthy and write soon and tell all.

Love, Hank

UNITED STATES ARMY ARTILLERY AND MISSILE CENTER
FORT SILL, OKLAHOMA

15 September, '68

Hi Sis!

Thanks a lot for your letters. They are really good. They show you are really growing up fast and loving life to the hilt. I am happy.

Here at Fort Sill, no news is good news. My orders still remain "Report to Ft. Meade, Maryland" after completion of training here. Some of my buddies, however, have received changes in their orders and they are going to the jolly green jungle right after this course.

… The first six weeks of this course was pretty much of a review of everything we did in Georgia. The last few weeks, however, have been, if not stupendously educational, at least unbelievably eye-opening. Some of the more interesting phases are classified, so mum's the word on that, but there are other areas like tactics, air defense systems, gunnery, etc., which in their own way contribute to a great broadening of one's horizons. Lots of "good to know" information, but at the same time "hope we don't have to employ" information.

Next, let me tell you about flight lessons. I have fifteen hours logged so far (need forty hours to qualify for federal license). Flying is really great! For Rosh Hashana I plan to fly down to Dallas (by myself!!!), park at the airport for two days, then return here on the 24th! I'll tell you, Deb, I don't know what I'd do if I wasn't doing something like this as an extra-curricular activity. I look forward to an average of an hour or so in the sky every day after classes.

Should I say hello to anyone for you in Dallas? Be more than happy to make a few phone calls for you and act as your personal "ambassador to the mainland."

Got to go now. Keep your letters coming. And always keep enjoying life.

Love, Hank

CHAPTER THREE

PETITIONING THE PENTAGON

A military prison is situated on the base in Fort George G. Meade, Maryland. I was assigned to the Special Processing Battalion that managed the prison and dealt with the needs of the inmates during the length of their incarceration.

When I first arrived on the base on October 14, 1968, I was unclear as to what my duties there would be. Eventually, because of my background as a law student, I was assigned to act as a defense attorney for the soldiers during their courts-martial. (In the army, an officer doesn't need a law degree, or any education in law for that matter, to be an attorney.)

It was ironic that my very first assignment was one in the profession that I had come to the army to escape. Nonetheless,

I did my work with complete dedication and defended the accused soldiers to the best of my ability. Typically, they were charged with stealing, fighting, being disrespectful to a superior, or being AWOL (Absent Without Leave; they had left the base without authorization and were thus accused of deserting the army).

I defended the soldiers by using a variety of technical defenses, and on numerous occasions the men were exonerated. Those who were found guilty usually received a maximum sentence of several months.

It seems that I was doing *too* good of a job as a defense attorney, and my superiors were not pleased that so many alleged offenders were let off the hook. Thus, after a short period of time, I was assigned to take the army's side and I became a prosecutor instead.

Although I got a fair number of convictions, this position didn't last long either. I eventually became a company commander of Headquarters Company, working underneath Lieutenant Colonel Robert B. Maucere, the Commanding Officer of the Special Processing Battalion. Headquarters Company administered to the needs of all the workers of the Special Processing Battalion. I had to ensure that everyone was housed and fed and received all the necessary provisions. In addition, I had to make sure that the men's sleeping quarters and recreational areas were orderly and properly equipped.

I continued my flight lessons in Fort Meade, and as in Fort Sill, they were always the highlight of my day. Although I was able to fly solo now, I had still not earned my federal license. A total of forty hours in the air is required for that, and slowly but surely, I found myself advancing towards that goal.

Towards the end of 1968, a good friend of mind, Paulo Perréro, informed me that lists were being drawn up for the next group of soldiers to be sent to Vietnam. Paulo, originally from Brazil, was a spirited fellow, and he wanted to be where the action was. He urged me to join him in volunteering to go to Vietnam. Although I wasn't quite as eager to be on the battlefield, I still felt that it was my duty to help protect the people there. After all, it was one of the reasons that I had signed up for the ROTC in the first place.

Therefore, I agreed to Paulo's plan, and after a short while we received orders to report for duty in April of 1969. It is customary for soldiers to receive several weeks furlough before they are dispatched to a combat zone, so I decided to visit my sister Debby who was studying in Israel during this interval.

There was only one problem. Because of the conflict and political unrest in the Middle East, the Department of Defense had decreed that active duty soldiers were prohibited from visiting the area. It was considered a dangerous region and they did not want the lives of their soldiers to be compromised.

Still, I refused to be deterred. I had resolved to visit my sister, and I was not about to give up on my plan. I spoke about my intentions endlessly, asking everyone on the base to help me find a way to visit her. I was confident that there was *some* way to make my trip possible.

One day, I was speaking to Sergeant Major Robert Longfellow, who was an assistant to my boss, Colonel Maucere. Longfellow was a career soldier who had served in the army for almost forty years and, as a sergeant major, had reached one of the highest ranks of a non-commissioned officer.

"Why don't you get hold of the person who wrote the regulation?" Longfellow suggested. "Whoever wrote the regulation will know how to get around it. The Pentagon is only thirty miles down the highway. I'm sure there's some way for you to get to the one who wrote it."

"Thanks," I said. "That's a great idea. Why didn't I think of it?"

I immediately began doing some research, relieved that there was finally something constructive for me to do to try to achieve my goal. After making some inquiries, I learned that the author of the regulation was Colonel H. Marks. He worked for Brigadier General Edward Bautz, Jr., who was the Director of Military Personnel Policies in the Pentagon.

After finally contacting Colonel Marks, I was told that I would have to write a petition establishing that, among other things, I would not be a security risk for the country; I would not wear my uniform during the trip; I would not take an inordinate amount of gold out of the U.S.; and I had a compelling reason for the General to make an exception and approve my request.

Once the petition was drawn up, I couldn't simply deliver it to General Bautz for his signature. In the military, everything must go through various channels. Therefore, the petition would have to be hand-carried through all the appropriate echelons. First, I would have to get the signature of my immediate boss, Colonel Maucere. Then, it would have to be signed by the Commanding Officer of Fort Meade *and* the Commanding General of First United States Army Headquarters, which was fortunately also located on the base. Finally, after these three signatures appeared on the document, I would be able to present it to General Bautz's office.

Considering the bureaucratic pace of military proceedings, the requirements for this petition were almost impossible to fulfill. Besides, even if I did accomplish all of this, no one could guarantee that my request would be granted.

My friends on the base believed that this was a futile endeavor, and they tried to dissuade me from even attempting to achieve what they considered the impossible. However, they hadn't realized just how stubborn and resolute I was, and they watched with some amusement as I began working on my petition with single-minded determination.

The petition was typed up by my clerk-typist in a military style document. (I drove him nearly nuts, as he had to retype it several times until it was "zero-defects.") I requested permission to travel to Israel to visit my sister from on or about March 1, 1969, until on or about March 26, 1969. I stated that I "have no intention of doing anything which could remotely be construed as adversely affecting the interests of the United States of America or the United States Army" and promised to return in "sufficient time" to report for duty to Vietnam on April 1, 1969.

With the document in hand, I went to Colonel Maucere's office. After saluting and asking for permission to speak, I presented the petition to him.

"So you want to go to Israel," he said, as he reviewed the document. "Isn't that the place where they have those pretty stones that are used to make jewelry and trinkets?"

"Sir, do you mean Eilat stones?" I asked.

"Whatever they are called," he said with a faint smile. "My wife just loves those stones."

"Sir," I said solemnly, "if I get to Israel, you can be sure that I will do my best to bring back some Eilat stones for you."

Colonel Maucere was pleased to hear this, and without further ado, he scrawled his name on the paper. I thanked him profusely, saluted, and headed towards the door.

"By the way, Webb," he called after me, "whenever you are ready to go to the Pentagon with your petition, you can use my staff car and my driver for the trip."

"Thank you, sir," I said. "I may take you up on that offer. I really appreciate it, sir."

My next stop was the office of the base commander. I was unable to see the commander, but his adjutant, a black female major, was authorized to sign the document for him.

For some reason, as soon as I stepped into her office, I sensed some hostility. We hadn't hit it off right, and she was unwilling to take any steps to make things easier for me.

"Look, Lieutenant," she said, "these things don't happen overnight. I must do various background checks to make sure that you are not a security risk. It will take some time for me to receive all the reports I need. And it's not like I have nothing else to do here. I will probably not have an answer for several weeks."

"Ma'am, you don't understand," I pleaded. "I don't *have* several weeks. I have orders to leave for Vietnam in April."

"I'll get to it when I get to it," she said, shrugging noncommittally.

After a couple of days, I called the major to see whether she had made any progress. "I told you," she said brusquely, "these things take time. You have to be patient."

After a number of delays, I was finally informed that there hadn't been any negative reports on the security checks, and my request had been approved. It was signed by a Captain C.D. Young who worked in that office.

I sighed in relief and hurried to present my petition to the First Army Headquarters. One of the secretaries was a Jewish lieutenant with whom I often ate breakfast in the mess hall. "Would you run this by the general for me?" I asked, after explaining the situation.

"Oh no," he said quickly. "You want to go to Israel? I'm not getting involved in this!"

I had no choice but to go to the general's office myself. Fortunately, I had some better luck there, and a sympathetic civilian secretary managed to get the petition signed by one of the general's aides.

At last, I was ready to go to the Pentagon. True to his word, Colonel Maucere allowed me to use his car and driver, and I climbed into the comfortable sedan, which had the colonel's flag attached on the outside. It was a short ride to the Pentagon, and as soon as we pulled up at the gate, the guard gave one glance at the vehicle, saluted, and immediately provided a preferred parking space and directions to the Personnel Policies Division.

I walked into the office of Colonel John Marks, the adjutant of Brigadier General Edward Bautz, Jr., who had drafted the regulation. Colonel Marks was sitting together with three other colonels, and I presented the petition to him.

Colonel Marks perused the document and then glanced up. "So you are from Fort Meade, eh?" he asked.

"Yes, sir," I replied.

"Aren't they running a sale on raincoats in the Quartermaster shop on your base?" he asked.

"Sir, I'm not aware of it," I said, "but if they are, what's your size, sir?"

Colonel Marks gave me his coat size and then asked, "What about the other gentlemen sitting in my office?" So I took down the sizes of the other three as well.

"Well, I'll need a couple of days," the colonel said, returning to the matter at hand. "When you come back, though, I would really appreciate it if you could get us those raincoats."

When I returned one week later, I had raincoats for all the colonels, except for the one I most wanted to please. The store had been out of the size Colonel Marks had requested, and I respectfully expressed my regret about the matter.

I handed the coats to the other three men and was pleasantly surprised when they all reimbursed me for the expense. Somehow, when I had paid for the purchase, I wondered whether I would ever see the money again and decided to consider it part of my traveling expenses to visit Debby.

"Well," Colonel Marks said when our transactions were completed, "the petition is not signed yet, but you will be hearing from me within several days."

I thanked the colonel for his time and left his office. As I made my way out of the Pentagon, I bumped into a Jewish colonel who worked there. Having inherited my father's outgoing personality, I struck up a conversation with him and soon found myself relating the purpose of my visit to the Pentagon.

"I wish you the best of luck," he said jovially. "I hope you get to visit your sister. And by the way, if your trip does get approved, it might be helpful for you to know that the Air Force runs a regular flight from Athens, Greece, to Israel. If you can get to Athens, perhaps you will be able to hop onto it. This flight is classified information, though," he added, "so if anyone will ask, I haven't told you anything."

I took down the flight information and thanked him for his assistance. "I'll definitely keep it in mind," I said, as I pocketed the piece of paper.

When I returned to the base, all my friends stopped me to ask whether the petition had been approved. "Oh, just forget about it!" they laughed when they heard what the colonel had said. "He forgot about it as soon as you stepped out of his office. We told you from the very beginning not to get your hopes up."

"I don't know why you're all so sure this is over," I said optimistically. "I still believe that I will make that trip to Israel and see my sister."

To my good fortune, and to my friends' disbelief, the colonel did not forget about me. As he had promised, I did hear from him several days later. On February 7, 1969, an order, signed by Colonel John Marks on behalf of Brigadier General Edward Bautz, Jr., came through on the teletype, authorizing Lieutenant Webb to travel from the East Coast of CONUS (Continental United States) to Israel and return in time for his overseas service on "space available travel by non-scheduled military aircraft..."

The clause referring to "space available travel" meant that I was authorized to travel on any military craft—be it an airplane, helicopter, submarine, or ship—that had extra space on board. Of course, this did not mean that a trip would be made especially for me, but if any military aircraft was heading in that direction, I could show my orders to the pilot, and if there was room, I would be welcome to hop along.

Needless to say, I was overjoyed! Clutching the orders to my chest, I ran around the base showing it to my friends. I didn't even bother acting smug or proclaiming that I had proven them all wrong. I was going to see Debby and I couldn't have been more excited.

Two weeks later, on February 21, I left Fort Meade, Maryland, for the very last time. I had a warm send-off from the many friends I had made during the four months that I had served on the base. One man I had worked closely with, my First Sergeant Eugene Hanson, presented me with an autographed picture. "Our association has been one of the most rewarding and enjoyable in my entire eighteen years of service," he wrote on the back of the photograph. "Much luck to you in future service and other endeavors."

I made a quick visit home to my parents in Waltham. Then, a week later, I packed a small suitcase and headed for McGuire Air Force Base in New Jersey. As I had pledged in my petition, I was wearing civilian clothes, since I was not permitted to travel in uniform during this trip.

After reaching the base, I learned that flights left regularly towards various European countries, but most of them were full. Since my orders were on a space available basis, I was told to await my turn, and I would be called.

Finally, after two nights of sleeping on airport benches, my name was called. A plane that was leaving for Spain had a vacant seat. Although Spain is quite some distance from my intended destination, it was definitely going in the right direction, so I quickly got on board.

As an officer of the United States Army, I was awarded some privileges, and I received excellent accommodations at the Officers' Club on the Spanish base. After a good night's sleep, I made some inquiries about the possibilities of further transportation. There was a submarine that was heading down the Mediterranean, but that wouldn't reach the Middle East region for some time. Finally, I settled on a flight to Italy, and from there, I eventually made my way to Athens, Greece.

Recalling the information I had received from the Jewish colonel at the Pentagon, I walked over to a restricted area from where American military flights departed. There was a small building located there, but I could not find a bell anywhere. Seeing no other option, I ignored the signs prohibiting intruders and opened the front door.

The door had not yet opened completely, when I spotted a Marine major sitting behind a desk. He glanced up in horror and looked at me as though I was poison.

"Get out of here! Get out!" he yelled.

"But, sir,-" I tried to explain.

"No but. Just get out! Now!"

It was quite clear that I had entered a secure area without prior authorization. The major was completely uninterested in whatever I had to say. I had no choice but to leave. I realized with regret that this was the end of my free ride via the United States Army.

Lugging my suitcase, I went over to the civilian side of the airport and approached the El Al counter. By now, after several days on the road, I was completely worn out. I just wanted to get to Israel, and get there fast.

"I'd like a ticket to Israel, please," I said to the woman behind the counter.

"Our last flight for today has already left," she said politely. "We don't have any flights this Saturday. You'll have to wait at least 24 hours."

"Oh, I can't wait that long," I said with some annoyance. "I need to get to Israel right now!"

"Why don't you try British Airways?" the woman asked helpfully, sensing my frustration. "They're in the next building."

I thanked her, picked up my luggage once again, and ran to the British Airways counter. "I'd like to purchase a ticket to Israel," I said breathlessly.

"There's a flight leaving in about ten minutes," I was told. "In fact, the passengers are already boarding."

"Great. How much is it?" I asked, pulling out a traveler's check.

"Oh, we don't accept that," the teller said, glancing at the check in my hand.

"What do you mean?" I asked, bewildered. "Travelers' checks are accepted all over the world!"

"I'm sorry, but I can only take Greek currency. There's a bank a couple of buildings away. You can exchange the check for Greek currency there."

"Okay," I said, "I'm leaving my luggage here by the counter. I'll be right back."

Following her directions, I ran to the bank as fast as my legs would take me. I quickly made the exchange and returned flushed and panting in record time.

Moments later, I had a ticket to Israel in my hand. The rest of the passengers had already boarded, and they were holding the Jetway just for me, as I rushed to get through customs.

"Passport, please," a man requested.

Since I only had to show my military orders until this leg of my journey, it took me a minute or so to dig up my passport. Finally, I handed it to him, waiting impatiently for him to wave me on.

"Hey, not so fast, young man," he said after glancing inside. "Where have you been for the last year? This passport was last stamped in Panama in 1968!"

"I've been in the United States. I guess it wasn't stamped when I reentered the country after my trip to South America."

"But how did you get into *this* country then?" he asked skeptically. "Or was it not stamped when you entered Greece as well?"

"Well, I've spent the past year with the United States Army," I explained. "I came to Greece on a military aircraft, so I didn't pass the regular airport customs."

The man looked at me doubtfully. It was quite a story, and he didn't know what to make of it. "Do you have any other I.D.?" he asked.

I hadn't pulled out my military I.D. initially, because I wasn't sure how he would react to a document of the U.S. Department of Defense. Now, however, I presented my military I.D. as well as my orders authorizing me to travel to Israel on military craft.

As soon as he saw the documents, he broke into a broad smile. "Why didn't you show this to me in the first place, sir?" he asked cheerfully. "Hurry up, now. The flight's waiting for you."

I was quickly ushered on board, where I was greeted by the not-so-friendly faces of my annoyed fellow passengers. They had been left waiting for at least fifteen minutes for me, the final passenger, who hadn't managed to get his act together in time.

Ignoring their long faces, I sighed in relief as I quickly took my seat. At this point, nothing could darken my mood. I was finally on a plane that was heading *directly* to Israel.

Fort George G. Meade
Maryland

7 February, '69
1045 Hrs

Shalom Debby!

Just a very quick note so say thanks for your faithful correspondence and also dig this: I'm coming to Israel in March!

Yessiree! Just received authorization from a Brigadier General in the Pentagon to travel outside the Western Hemisphere, and particularly to Israel, just to visit you!

More details as soon as I make more definite plans.

Can't leave here much before 1 March, and must be in Vietnam by 1 April, so it'll be a tight schedule. …

Love and Kisses. I'll write more soon.

Hank

Fort George G. Meade
Maryland

11 November, '68

Dear Debby,

Thanks for yours (sic) of the 3rd Nov. and thanks also for writing the date in English for me.

You started your letter by saying, "By the time you receive this there should be a new President-elect of the U.S. ..." Well, now that your profound prediction has come true, what comments do you have to make? As for me, while President-elect Nixon might not have been my first choice, as far as I can determine, the election was all fair and square, and this is apparently what most state populations want. ...

I am convinced now ... that to allow the Communists to take over nations which are trying to provide a government where the people will not be afraid to bring their grievances... to just sit back and allow this to happen when several of these small countries have asked for our help, seems to me foolhardy. We are in this sense our brother's keeper. I think, even though the brother we are trying to help is not always doing exactly what we approve of (I refer to corruption in gov't, and "paper" democracies). At least it's a gov't which is attempting to go in a direction which would eventually ensure more individual freedom, private business incentive, protection of the right to dissent, demonstrate, etc. ...

Debby, I have a new job!! I am no longer working as trial counsel in the legal section for the battalion. I am now:

1/Lt. Hank Webb
Commanding Officer
Headquarters Company

Detention Detachment
Special Processing Battalion
Fort George G. Meade, Maryland 20755

...and I'll thank you to call me SIR!

Yep, it's a great big challenge for me. I have more than 100 enlisted men and about 30 officers under me. I don't have direct responsibility for their performance at work during the day, however. My main concern is their overall welfare after duty hours. I am setting up counseling hours, trying to improve the day room (recreation area), and also trying to shape up the men and the billets. The billets are in bad shape ... I've held three inspections and chewed [the men] out twice. One time I threatened to hold everyone here for the weekend unless they straightened out fast. I noticed some improvement Friday, so I let everyone go on condition they come back ready to really work hard. ...

Deb, please tell me more about the military situation where you are. I am very concerned for your safety, as is everyone at home. ...

Your statement "Israel is our home and our only home and the only place we aren't 'wandering Jews'" has a ring of truth to it; but don't we have as much right to live anywhere else in the world as the next guy? If every Jew decided to come to Israel, wouldn't we all be conceding a right to exist free from harm in other parts of the world? Freedom must be lived, to be kept alive, don't you think? ...

When will we see you, Deb?

Oh yes, the plane lessons. ... I took the federal exam the other day, and logged another hour in the air. Only about 10 more hours to go!!

Write soon and stay safe and happy.

ILY. Hank

CHAPTER FOUR

SHABBOS BY FORCE

*G*rowing up, my sister Debby had always been different from the rest of our family. She was the only Jewish kid in her class in public school, but she had many friends from Hebrew School and her best friend was *shomer* Shabbos. Thus, Debby was exposed to an observant lifestyle from early on, and she became very drawn to it. Additionally, the passing of our little brother, Joshua, had a great impact on her and changed her outlook on life. She was exceptionally strong-minded and independent and was completely unfazed by the fact that none of her family members shared her interest in such a different way of life.

I particularly remember an incident that occurred during one of our annual camping trips. It was in the summer of 1965, just one month short of Debby's sixteenth birthday, when we left home, hoping to reach Mexico and Guatemala. After our departure, we stopped at Harriman State Park in New York to spend a couple of days there. When my father wanted to resume our trip, Debby refused to get into the car.

"It's Shabbos today, Dad," she said. "We're not allowed to travel on Shabbos."

As was his practice when confronting conflict, my father handled the matter as though it were a legal problem. "Look, Debby," he said, "people are entitled to their individual beliefs. If you decide not to travel on Shabbos, that's fine. But right now, you are traveling with a group. All the other people in the group are eager to continue the trip and stick to our preplanned schedule. When you are alone, you can do as you please, but in this case, majority rules. You can't hold up the whole family just because *you* don't want to travel on Saturday."

But Debby was adamant. "I'm not stopping you from driving away," she said. "You can do as you please, but I'm not getting into the car. Shabbos is a day of rest, and the Torah says that it is forbidden to travel on Shabbos."

At that time, I was twenty-three years old. I was feeling very frustrated that at this stage in my life, I was still traveling on vacation with my family and undecided about my future. I believed that I should already have been leading a life of my own. For some reason, I directed much of my anger towards my father. I jumped at the opportunity to take Debby's side and vent some of my dissatisfaction.

"Dad," I piped up, "you talk about majority rules and all that, but Debby has a source for her argument, which is the Torah, so her point of view carries more weight, After all, when there's a clear-cut law, what individuals want is irrelevant. And what's the big deal anyway? We'll stay here for one extra day. It doesn't really make that much of a difference."

Debby gave me a small smile of gratitude and turned to my father. "You can do as you wish," she said quietly, "but I'm staying here."

By now, it was quite clear to my father that he could not convince his strong-headed daughter to change her mind. Respectfully, but firmly, she declared her refusal to travel on Shabbos. In the end, the family agreed to stay in Harriman State Park for an extra day.

But Debby's desire to lead an observant life was not, as some members of the family assumed, merely a temporary teenage phase. She only became more committed as she got older. Rabbi Aaron Kra, our rabbi in Waltham, was very supportive of Debby and began studying Torah with her on Shabbos. Later, she also developed close ties with the Bostoner Rebbe, who was instrumental in bringing thousands of lost Jewish souls closer to *Yiddishkeit*.

The Bostoner Rebbe, Grand Rabbi Levi Yitzchok Horowitz, is well known for his *hachnosis orchim* to everyone, especially students from all over the Boston area. For many, this was their first introduction to Yiddishkeit. The Bostoner provided a sounding board and advice not readily available to them elsewhere. In this environment, Debby felt comfortable exploring her own growing interest in *Yiddishkeit*. She frequently consulted the Rebbe on issues pertaining to religion, and before long, she began spending Shabbos with the Rebbe's family almost every week. My parents were a bit bewildered by this arrangement, but she was determined to go, and they couldn't help but notice her radiant face each time she returned from one of her visits there.

Although I didn't understand Debby's passion for religion back then, she still had a very special place in my heart, and I tried my best to help her whenever I had a chance. One Pesach she wanted to join the Rebbe's family for the *seder* on the first night, after our own family *seder* at a cousin's home in Brookline. However, my parents insisted that she return to be with her family for the second day. Since she would obviously not ride home, I volunteered to accompany her for the three-hour walk back so that she would not have to give up on the longed-for *yom tov* experience at the Rebbe's house.

During her senior year in high school, Debby asked my parents for permission to join a year-long work/study Bnei Akiva program in Israel. My mother felt that she was too young for such a trip. "You can go for your third year of college," she told Debby, "if you promise to return home to complete your studies and graduate."

After graduating from high school, Debby enrolled in Brandeis University, located in our hometown, Waltham, Massachusetts. Named after Justice Louis Dembitz Brandeis (1856-1941), the first Jewish Supreme Court Justice, the university offers courses in Judaic studies in addition to its regular curriculum. A number of Debby's religious friends also studied there, and so, within the close-knit group, she was able to continue her quest for spiritual growth.

At the time, Brandeis University gave college credits to students who participated in a third year study program at Hebrew University in Jerusalem. Debby, who was still eager to visit the Holy Land, signed up.

After two years at Brandeis, Debby finally left for Israel in July of 1968. When I boarded the plane in Greece on Friday, March 7, 1969, Debby had been living in Israel for almost eight months. Despite my busy schedule, I had kept up a faithful correspondence with her during that time and was happy to read her enthusiastic letters about the joys of living in Jerusalem.

Now, as the British Airways plane approached the airstrip at Lod Airport, I took my first glance at my sister's beloved new homeland. I couldn't see much since it was already dark outside. After the plane landed, I tried to be patient and not jostle those around me, as I eagerly made my way towards the exit. I could hardly contain my excitement at my imminent reunion with my dear sister.

I hailed a *sherut* (taxi) with three other young men from my flight. To our dismay, we learned that fees in Israel are almost doubled on weekends. We resigned ourselves to the fact that we would be parting with a considerable amount of cash as we each gave our destination to the driver.

Israeli taxi drivers are known for their incessant chatter and persistent, pointed questions, and the man behind the wheel of our cab proved himself loyal to the preservation of this image. He bombarded us with questions about our personal life and the purpose of our visit. After spending only a short period of time in the vehicle, the driver knew all about my upcoming tour of duty in Vietnam and my wish to see my sister, who had recently become *dati*, or religious.

With one hand on the wheel, his mouth in constant motion, and an occasional glance at the road, the driver somehow managed to deposit my three companions safely at their destinations. Then, as the third passenger slammed the passenger door shut, he turned to me with a smile. "So, you want to go to Yerushalayim, eh?" he asked.

"Yes," I said. "I already gave you my sister's address."

"You know," he said, as he expertly guided the car back onto the busy road, "I will take you to a better place."

I looked at him in confusion. "No, it's fine. I really don't want to do any sightseeing now. I want to go directly to Jerusalem."

"No, no, I'll take good care of you. I'll take you someplace else."

Now I knew that Israelis are known for their *chutzpah*, but this was, quite simply, outrageous! Since when does a driver decide his passenger's destination?

"Don't you understand?" I asked irritably. "I want you to take me to that address in Jerusalem. I want to see my sister. I want to see her now. Today."

But my pleas fell on deaf ears, as the driver insisted that he had "a better place" to take me to. He gave me no choice at all in the matter; I was simply a prisoner in his cab. To my dismay, he soon pulled up before the Malon Savoy, or Savoy Hotel, in Tel Aviv, all the while assuring me that "everything will be fine."

Not only was I nowhere close to my intended destination, but I also had to pay the hefty "weekend surcharge" that the driver demanded. He paid no heed to my frustration, and after a wave of his hand and a parting "Shalom," he left me standing at the curb with my luggage.

While the driver never bothered to explain why he hadn't taken me to the destination I had requested, I was able to guess the reason for his actions after spending some time in Israel. Since I had mentioned that my sister was religious, he probably assumed that she was living in a religious neighborhood, and he was afraid to drive there after dark on Friday night. Apparently, he didn't want to expose himself and his vehicle to some zealous, stone-throwing Yerushalmi Jews who he thought might attack anyone violating the laws of the holy Shabbos.

As I surveyed my surroundings, I noticed a nearby disco that was filled with many partying young men and women. Assuming they were Arabs, I didn't give them a second glance, but instead, picked up my luggage and entered the hotel. There was a guest book open on the check-in counter, and I picked up a pen to sign in.

"No, no! You don't have to sign the book," the woman behind the counter said quickly. "We'll just take you right to your room."

I shrugged my shoulders and put down the pen. "All right," I said. "I'd just like to make one phone call before settling into my room."

Private phones in hotel rooms weren't common back then, and I wished to let Debby and my parents know of my safe arrival.

"I'm sorry," the woman said apologetically, "but you can't use the phone today. It's Shabbos. You will have to wait until tomorrow night."

I tried putting forth my most winning smile. "Aw, come on," I said. "It won't take me more than a minute. Just one quick call."

"I'm sorry. It's not allowed."

I was too tired to argue. I went to my room and fell into bed. I was so worn out that I fell asleep instantly, feeling confident that I would take care of matters first thing in the morning.

I woke up the next day feeling rested and refreshed. I dressed quickly and hurried down to the lobby. "I'd like to use the phone, please," I requested politely.

There was another woman standing behind the counter now, but she was just as stubborn as the one I had met the previous night. "I'm sorry," she said. "This is a religious hotel, and we don't allow guests to make calls on Shabbos."

"Oh, I won't be long at all," I said amiably, trying to charm her into making an exception for me. "Really. Just a quick call."

She shook her head. "Why don't you go out and take a walk," she suggested. "The scenery is beautiful here and the beach is only a short distance away. Come back at 12:00; we'll be serving a very nice lunch then."

I left the lobby, trying to make sense of the latest events. Since I had arrived in Israel, no one was interested in what I wanted to do. The taxi driver didn't bother to listen to me, but took me to wherever he pleased, and the people at the hotel were expecting me to follow their ridiculous rules about not using the phone on Saturday! I had yet to bump into one of the enchanting people that Debby raved about in her letters.

Taking the advice of the woman behind the counter, I went to the beach and strolled along the shore. The view was indeed breathtaking, and I was soothed by the warm air and glistening water. I felt a sense of serenity and joy wash over me, and by the time I returned to the hotel for lunch, I was humming a tune and walking with a bounce in my step.

When I walked into the hotel dining room, I found about twenty people sitting around a long table that had been beautifully prepared for the Shabbos meal. I greeted the other guests and sat down on an empty chair. As soon as everyone was seated, a man at one end of the table recited Kiddush over a cup of wine. The melodious chant struck a chord inside me, and it brought back some warm, distant memories of the few occasions that I had taken part in a traditional holiday meal.

The others at the table were all observant Jews and were familiar with the strange menu of the Shabbos meal. I was obviously an outsider, and the people tried to make me feel comfortable. They were very friendly and welcoming and inquired about the reason for my visit. Sharing the meal with these strangers evoked some sort of kinship, and I soon found myself relating my entire story —again!

After the meal, I continued chatting with the guests through the afternoon. The hours passed quickly and soon it was time for *havdalah*. Shabbos was over at last. It had been an interesting day for me, since I had never experienced Shabbos to such an extent. I had spent the entire Shabbos in an observant environment, had partaken in a *seudah* with *frum* people, and had not used the telephone the entire day. Of course, all this had not been done by choice, and so I came to refer to that day as "Shabbos by force."

After *havdalah*, I was finally permitted to use the telephone. I contacted Debby and arranged to meet her at the central bus station in Yerushalayim. And so, more than twenty-four hours after arriving in Israel, I was at last reunited with my dear sister. Gil Eisenbach, a young man she was seriously dating, had also come with her to meet me.

Gil's father was originally from Israel, but Gil had been raised in the United States and had recently come to Israel to learn in a *yeshivah*. He was very devoted to his studies, and unlike the young people I usually hung out with, he had a serious air about him. I quickly discovered, though, that he also had a good sense of humor.

Overall, Gil made a very good impression on me, and he seemed to be a nice, considerate young man. I was very happy for Debby and hoped that the relationship would turn out well. I knew how much she wanted to find a partner in life who shared her ideals and values and was equally committed to establishing a true Jewish home.

As we began wandering through the city's streets together, I said, "Wow! I didn't realize the Arabs have so much freedom here."

"Where did you see Arabs?" Debby asked in surprise. At that time, so soon after Israel had gained its independence, the Arabs still kept their distance.

"Oh, I saw them partying in some nightclub in Tel Aviv last night," I explained.

"Those were probably Jews," Debby said.

"But they were riding in cars and going in and out of restaurants," I said in confusion. "Jews in Israel don't do that on Shabbos, so they must have been Arabs!"

I took it for granted that in the Holy Land all Jews were religious, and it came as a shock when Debby informed me that this was not so. "There are all kinds of Jews in Israel, just like in America. Some are religious and some are as far from that as you can possibly be. Not everyone is sensitive to the opportunity to grow spiritually in Eretz Yisrael."

We continued walking together until late at night. When we were both too tired to take another step, Debby brought me to her flat. She had graciously arranged for me to sleep in her room near the university, while she moved in with one of her friends who had an apartment nearby.

The next day, Debby introduced me to many other students, and I was surprised to find myself enjoying the company of Debby's friends immensely. In truth, I had previously been prejudiced against people who led such a lifestyle. I recalled driving through Boston's streets with some family members as a young boy. We passed some observant Jews walking home from *shul* and one of my relatives had wrinkled his nose with distaste.

"Look at those people. They are so old-fashioned," he had commented with an air of superiority. "They live as though they are still in the ghetto."

From then on, I had looked with some negativity upon religious Jews. Now, however, after spending time with Debby's crowd, I realized that my assumptions about observant people were completely unfounded. I had never had a chance to mingle with them before, and my encounter with them in Israel turned out to be a very positive experience. Everyone was very pleasant and forthcoming, not at all like the dour, cheerless group I had expected, and I came to admire their commitment to their beliefs.

Debby took some time off from school to take me around the country and visit some popular tourist spots. We had a wonderful time and stayed up late every night, conversing together. I sometimes played the guitar, and we would reminisce about our childhood years.

When the next Shabbos rolled around, I was still in the company of Debby and her friends. After my memorable "Shabbos by force" at the Malon Savoy, I now considered myself somewhat of an "expert" and had an easier time following the various "rules." Unlike the previous week, though, my Shabbos now began at sundown on Friday and it included **three** *seudahs*.

Shabbos at the Malon Savoy had been, at times, rather frustrating, but in Debby's company, it was a day that I cherished for months thereafter. As soon as the candles were lit, an aura of holiness and peace permeated the entire apartment. I was moved by the warm atmosphere at the Shabbos table, and I came away with a completely new outlook on observant life.

As I watched Debby during my second week in Israel, I envied the spirituality that she had brought into her everyday life. Here she was, a regular university student with a large circle of friends, leading a life that was, in many ways, very much like that of other people her age. Nonetheless, each day was filled with meaning, and she had managed to find that inner peace that had, so far, eluded me.

Another eye-opener was watching Debby and Gil spend time together. I was struck by the deep mutual caring they had for each other, despite their observance of no *negiah*. Their dating relationship was in stark contrast to the superficial dating experiences I had had over the years.

Before long, my time in Israel was up, and I had to start preparing for my trip back home. Since I would again be traveling on a roundabout route aboard military aircraft, I had to leave on March 18 to allow several days for the journey to the United States.

Before I left Jerusalem, Debby presented me with a *tefilas haderech*. She and Gil explained the meaning and significance of this special prayer to me, as they blessed me that I arrive safely in Vietnam and return home unharmed after I completed my tour of duty.

Gil also gave me a package to deliver to his parents in Wilmington, Delaware. Since my pilot's license was due to arrive in the mail any day, I was hoping to deliver it myself. I missed my frequent excursions in the small planes I piloted and looked forward to renting a small aircraft and spending some time in the clouds before I departed for Vietnam.

At last, it was time to bid farewell to my sister and her friends. I took a taxi to Lod Airport, hoping to get onto the Air Force flight that departed from there to Turkey, and then continue to Athens. After making my way through customs, I jumped over a low iron gate to get into the restricted area. In the end, I learned that the flight was delayed for twenty-four hours, and I would have to return the following night.

Thus, I spent another day in the Holy Land before returning to the airport. Since security in Israel was very tight, I could not know in advance when and from where the flight would leave. "Wait here and someone will call you when it's time to leave," I was told.

I waited for several hours until I was finally called to board. I sat into a vacant seat and soon we were in the air. As I watched the lights of Israel fading away, I reflected on the life that Debby and her friends led. There was a purpose and quality to it that I could not help but admire.

My mind drifted back to an incident that had occurred shortly after I graduated from Boston University. It was during the summer of 1964, when I was temporarily employed at Chrysler Corporation in Detroit and shared a small apartment with my friend Mike Chertok in the city.

One glorious Sunday, I went to the beach with Mike and another friend. We were having a great time splashing about in the roped off area that had been designated safe for swimming. We were feeling young and invincible and foolishly believed that we must do something reckless in order to *really* have fun.

"Hey, do you see that out there?" our friend asked, pointing to a buoy that was bobbing on the water in the distance. "Let's see if we can swim all the way there and back."

It was a dare that we could not refuse without losing the respect of our friend, and so Mike and I readily agreed. We ducked under the safety rope and began swimming toward it.

In the water, everything appears to be much closer than it actually is, and it soon became apparent that the buoy was much farther out than we had originally believed. Still, none of us would admit defeat. Ignoring our aching arms and legs, we continued swimming doggedly toward our target.

At last, the marker was only several feet away. As soon as my two friends reached it, they turned around and began heading back to shore. I was completely out of breath, and as I approached the buoy, I decided to touch it and rest for a moment before following my friends back to the beach.

I reached out to grab hold of it, but it was covered with slimy, green algae. My hand slipped right off and I went under. I hadn't expected this to happen and was unprepared for my sudden dip. I swallowed some water as I went down, and when I came back up, I was sputtering and unable to catch my breath. I tried calling to my friends for help, but my voice would not project. They were already some distance ahead when, luckily, Mike looked over his shoulder to check on my progress. He immediately realized that I was struggling in the water and gasping for air. By now, I had gone under several times and was barely keeping afloat. Mike hurriedly swam back, caught me, and towed me all the way to shore. Once they got me safely onto the sand, my friends began pumping the excess water out of my body, and after several critical minutes, I was finally breathing regularly again.

It had been a very, very close call, and I was quite shaken up. After coming so close to death, I felt compelled to question the value of life. "Why am I still here?" I wondered. "Would it have mattered if I had died? What is the purpose of life?"

For several days, these questions weighed heavily on my mind. I didn't know the answers to them, and eventually I pushed them away. Life continued as usual.

Now, after spending almost two weeks in Debby's company, it was clear that she had indeed found a purpose to her life. She was not merely going about her daily activities aimlessly. She had firm beliefs and was obviously working to reach some personal goals that she had set for herself. Her life had meaning, and I envied her for that.

I was shaken out of my reverie as the plane approached Adana, Turkey. Although I had to focus now on making my way to the United States, I knew without a doubt that I would be spending more time dwelling on the purpose of my life, or the lack thereof, in the very near future.

As planned, I continued on to Athens and then took several connecting flights, until I finally landed in McGuire Air Force Base on March 23. When I was finally back in Waltham, I learned that my orders had changed. Instead of reporting at McGuire Air Force Base on April 3 for deployment to Vietnam, I now had until April 10.

After I came home, my parents were eager to hear my impressions of Gil Eisenbach. They hadn't objected to Debby spending Shabbos with the Bostoner Rebbe again and again, but now that she was seriously considering an engagement to a *yeshivah* student and a permanent relocation to Israel, they were distraught. They were afraid that she was alienating herself from the family and worried that she would one day have children who wouldn't be able to communicate with their own grandparents, since they would speak Hebrew, which was a foreign language to them.

I tried my best to reassure them and gave them a very positive report, praising Gil's pleasant character and fine intellect. My words calmed them to some extent, and they resigned themselves to the fact that Debby was set on leading a life very different from theirs.

To my disappointment, my pilot's license did not arrive until the day before my departure. By then, it was too late to take my little flying adventure, and I had to ship Gil's package to his parents, instead of delivering it personally to them.

On Thursday, April 10, 1969, I appeared as ordered at McGuire Air Force Base. In my uniform once more, my mind swirled with thoughts of the coming months. I hoped to secure a good post and be able to serve my country well. I feared the dangers that I was sure to encounter and prayed for a safe return.

And yet, amidst all these turbulent emotions, there was a soft voice whispering in my ear. A little spark was slowly growing brighter inside me, as the memory of a Shabbos table continued to tug at my heart. Eventually, the soft voice would become more persistent, and the little spark would burst into flame. My trip to Israel had lasted not quite two weeks, but its impact would remain for years to come.

9 March, 1969

Sunday

Safe with Debby in Jerusalem!

Mission accomplished, folks, and boy oh boy is it ever great to be here. Debby was about as enthusiastic as I think I've ever seen her when she flung her arms around me last night at the [bus station]. She was with Gil, who seems like everything Debby wrote about him. I really haven't had much time to talk with him, though. The three of us took a bus to Debby's dorm after walking around Yerushalayim for a while, talking and interrupting each other incessantly and stopping only briefly to sip hot chocolate and eat some pastry.

Today is Sunday, the first working day of the week, and it feels exactly like Monday back in the States. Construction crews are busy on a building going up next to Deb's dorm, the buses are crowded and all shops are open for business. It feels good to be in the majority class of the population rather than in the minority. Here, to say "The Jews this or that" attracts no attention whatsoever; to say "Jew" over a cup of coffee in a Boston or Waltham restaurant might raise a look or two. Don't you agree?

Deb has vacated her room so I can sleep in it this week, and she will stay one room down the hall with one of her girlfriends. Isn't that nice of her? It means I don't have to pay hotel bills, I get to see Deb more, and I get to talk with the Hebrew Univ. students more.

Yesterday evening it was somewhat tense in Jerusalem. Soldiers are all over the streets and as you know, they carry Israeli-made machine guns as well as weapons made elsewhere. … I've seen the U.S. Army style combat boots, only they don't bother polishing them here.

… The recent bombings here have touched none of us. The army shot down one Russian-made MiG-21 over the Sinai Desert yesterday, and the Egyptian pilot parachuted to safety. The Israelis took him to a hospital here, I think. This is truly a country which lives by the golden rule it seems, although Gen. Moshe Dayan, according to today's paper, says if the attacks continue, "They will have to get the lesson they deserve to bring them out of their stupor." Hoping for peace here is like hoping for a million dollars to appear before my eyes in the next 60 seconds, but what else is there to do but hope and pray?

Love to all,
Hank

19 March, '69

Dear Debby (and Gil, too),

Well, we're finally moving at about 9 p.m. tonight. I know we were supposed to leave last night, but now do you see why it's a good thing you didn't wait until the plane took off? It was delayed 24 hrs in Turkey, so Izzy Lurman, the guy you both met last night, and I stayed at the Hotel Avia in Lod and toured some more of Tel Aviv today. (I didn't want to bother you by calling to say I'd be here another day, because really it's about time you two had some time together without me, and also, we'd already said our goodbyes.)

…

Well, in 40 minutes I should be in Turkey. I can't say how long it will take to get back to Boston …

All for now. I'll give all your best, etc. to all I see.

Love, Hank

CHAPTER FIVE

ENTERING THE WAR ZONE

I arrived at Ben Hoa Airfield in Vietnam at about 0500 hours on Saturday morning, April 12. The plane, which had departed from the West Coast, was filled to capacity with soldiers who were going to various stations all over Vietnam. After the plane landed, we couldn't merely disembark, but we were instructed to run all the way to the building that was situated next to the runway. We would be exposed on the open tarmac, vulnerable to enemy fire, and it was important to run for cover as quickly as possible. Although no one shot at us as we jumped off the plane, we followed the directive regardless. We had entered a war zone, and one had to remain careful and alert at all times.

The first thing that hit me was the unbearable heat and humidity. Although it was still so early in the morning, it was already stifling. I would soon learn that the "normal" temperature during daylight hours is between eighty and one hundred degrees Fahrenheit!

The new arrivals were ordered to climb onto fortified transport buses and were escorted by a military convoy to a base in Long Binh. There, we were issued jungle fatigues, jungle boots, steel helmets, and other gear. Once we had all our supplies and equipment, we were assigned to bunks in an outdoor area.

The base was teeming with thousands of newly arrived military personnel. At this time, we had no idea where we would be stationed, or what our duties there would be. There were loudspeakers set up all over the area, and the names of soldiers were constantly being announced. We had to wait for our names to be called, and then we would receive our assignments.

I was bleary-eyed and exhausted from my lengthy trip. After all, I had traveled halfway around the world in the past two days. I fell into my bunk and dozed off, but after a short nap I awoke to listen to the names that were announced. I hoped that I wouldn't have to wait too long to hear mine. I was eager to learn where I would be stationed and looked forward to getting settled.

I waited until the following evening. On Sunday, April 13, at around 1900 hours (7:00 p.m.), I finally received my orders. I learned that I would be going to Da Nang, about 300 miles north, where I would join the 26th General Support Group. My flight was scheduled to leave Long Binh at 0330 hours (3:30 a.m.) on the morning of April 14.

I experienced mixed emotions as I waited with the other soldiers. On one hand, I felt excited and eager to begin my work; at the same time, though, a great fear had settled in the pit of my stomach, knowing that I was heading into battle. Not knowing what the coming days held in store, I spent the final hours in Long Binh sending heartfelt letters to my family in Waltham and to Debby and Gil in Israel.

As I was preparing for my departure, I learned that I would be traveling aboard a C-130. This plane has four large engines and is extraordinarily powerful. It is really heavy duty and can carry tons of weight in material and passengers. Moreover, the C-130 is very maneuverable, almost like a small plane, and can dive, climb, and stall. The only drawback is its speed—it doesn't fly fast at all. (Incidentally, the C-130 was used several years later, in 1976, by Israeli commandos during the famous raid on Entebbe—when they freed more than 100 airline passengers who were being held hostage in Uganda by Palestinian and West German guerrillas.)

I boarded this monstrous aircraft together with a number of other men and soon we were in the air. After a short trip, just as we were approaching the landing strip in Da Nang, the plane was fired upon. Unfortunately, I experienced firsthand one of the amazing feats this enormous bird can perform. Without warning, it suddenly stood up on its tail and shot skyward on full throttle. The blood drained from my head to my feet, and the strong gravity forces made it seem as though I weighed twice my normal weight. After leveling off at a safer altitude, the pilot circled for a second approach. Luckily, the plane landed without further incident, after, I assume, our artillery silenced the enemy position.

Once again, we jumped onto the tarmac with our gear and scrambled for cover. We boarded a bulletproof bus and were transported from the airport to the compound in Da Nang. The entire area was surrounded by barbed wire and there were piles of sandbags stacked everywhere. Since this was farther north than Long Binh, more protective gear was needed in this location, and security in general was very tight.

The base in Da Nang was enormous, like a miniature city, and there were dozens of units stationed in different areas. For us newcomers, it was an incredible sight to see thousands of American soldiers, from various branches and battalions, walking around.

I dragged my luggage to my newly assigned hut—or hooch, as we called it. The hooch contained eight bunk-beds and was shared by sixteen officers. (The enlisted soldiers did not receive such privileged quarters; they slept in large barracks, each of them housing dozens of men.)

In addition to the oppressive heat, the soldiers in Vietnam were also plagued by swarms of insects that circled at night. Thus, each bed came equipped with mosquito netting. The net enclosed the bed on all sides, like a tent, and once a solider was settled for the night, he zipped it closed.

I unpacked my belongings and put them away in the wall and foot lockers that were allotted to each soldier. I quickly learned the importance of keeping *everything* locked away at all times. Though there were some incidents of thievery among the troops, we all had to watch out for the Vietnamese women who cleaned our rooms. When they swept the hooch, more than just dirt disappeared. Frequently, whatever had been left laying around would be gone by the time we returned. Then, if anyone tried to question the women about the whereabouts of a missing item, they would shrug their shoulders and shake their heads apologetically. "No Engli. No Engli," they'd say. They conveniently used the language barrier to ward off all questions.

On my second day in Da Nang, I was assigned to work as a Personnel Service Officer in the office of Brigadier General John G. Gunn. I didn't work for the general directly, but under the supervision of his immediate subordinate, Major Stepp. I was in charge of supervising incoming and outgoing communications. I handled requests for equipment, supplies, and other matters, and sent them through the proper channels. Similarly, when orders for various regulations or reassignments came in, I would make sure that they were distributed to the appropriate lower commands, and collect written statements that the orders had been fulfilled. The job required good organizational skills, which I was still learning at that point. I am rather easygoing by nature and occasionally failed to meet an expected deadline.

In truth, I was rather disappointed to be stuck at this job. Only rarely did I make use of my extensive training as a Signal officer, although I officially also held M.O.S. of Signal Equipment Maintenance Officer. I had come to Vietnam to make a difference and help in the war effort with my expertise, and I desperately wanted to do something worthwhile. I felt that my skills were being wasted.

Shortly after I arrived in Da Nang, on May 1, 1969, I was promoted from First Lieutenant to Captain. Exactly one year had passed since I first began active duty, and as my performance had been satisfactory throughout, I was automatically promoted on this date. Afterwards, I went down to the Post Exchange to buy the appropriate insignia to attach to my uniform.

Although I was working in a relatively safe environment, this did not mean that I was out of danger. Mortar attacks during the night were common, and it was always a treat to sleep through the night undisturbed. Sometimes, even when there were no direct hits, the attacks resulted in injuries, and we were confronted with the realities of war on a regular basis.

Attacks did not come only during the night. One day, as I was walking near our headquarters building, an incoming rocket exploded about six yards away, forming a large crater in the ground. I had heard the whistling sound of its approach and hit the ground just moments before the explosion. Although I was hit by some shrapnel, I wasn't seriously injured. Nevertheless, it was an emotionally traumatic event, and for many years I would dive for cover each time I heard a loud, blasting sound. Even today, thirty-five years later, I flinch and get flashbacks when hearing noises that remind me of combat sounds.

I would not only be haunted by sounds, though, but by sights, too. A friend of mine worked in a morgue on base where the bodies of dead soldiers would be embalmed and placed in body bags for the journey home. One day I visited him there. Nothing could have prepared me for the gruesome, shocking sight of bodies with missing limbs and heads without bodies. I felt sick to my stomach and remained queasy for days thereafter.

Fortunately, there were some bright points, too. Although I didn't enjoy my position on the general's staff very much, there was one task that I always looked forward to. Every two weeks or so, I would travel into the city of Da Nang, accompanied by an armed guard. We crossed the river between our base and the city on one of the ferries run by the Marines. I carried a briefcase that was filled with payroll vouchers, and it was my duty to exchange it at the bank and carry back stacks of Vietnamese cash, or "scrip," that was used to pay the troops.

This bi-weekly excursion provided me with a unique opportunity to observe everyday life in this foreign, exotic city. There were always dozens of bicycles on the street; a considerable number of motor scooters; and only an occasional automobile. I looked with interest upon the small, one-story huts that lined the roads and watched the men, women, and children go about their everyday lives. Although I was saddened by the acute poverty I witnessed, it was a relief to escape from my monotonous desk job on base.

Since the bank was not supplied with any modern, sophisticated equipment, I always had to wait a long time while the tellers counted the vouchers and the money by hand. When we were both finally satisfied with the calculations, I filled the briefcase with the "scrip" and returned with the guard to our base.

Another anticipated event was my weekly language classes. Wanting to take something positive out of the time spent in Vietnam, I had decided to learn the local language. There was a trailer on base, where the army had set up a makeshift library for the soldiers. A Vietnamese librarian was employed there, and I arranged for weekly language lessons with her. Before long, my vocabulary grew to include a number of words.

During this time, I often reflected on the stark differences of lifestyle between the men on base and Debby's religious friends. With rare exceptions, the soldiers led a life that was devoid of any real value or meaning. While I tried using my spare time in the army constructively, by earning a pilot's license in Oklahoma and studying a new language in Vietnam, for most of the other guys, every off-duty minute was spent dozing, drinking, carousing, or just wasting time. After living briefly in an observant environment in Israel, the emptiness and shallowness of their lives became more apparent than ever.

Several months after my arrival in Da Nang, during the spring of 1969, I was overjoyed to learn of Debby's engagement to Gil Eisenbach. I knew that, together with Gil, Debby would be able to lead the kind of life she so fervently desired and establish a true Jewish home. The couple would have to endure a long engagement before their marriage, however, since Debby was scheduled to return home after her exams in Israel and complete her final year of studies at Brandeis University, as she had promised my parents. Thus, their wedding would take place only in the spring of 1970, after my return to the States.

I had been very positively influenced by Debby during our time together in Israel, and I kept up a regular correspondence with her. While still in Da Nang, I became increasingly interested in leading a more spiritual life. I was not yet ready to observe the Shabbos, but I began leading services in the Air Force Chapel on base on Friday night and Shabbos morning.

In early August, when I first instituted the weekly services, only a handful of men attended, but to my delight, our "congregation" soon grew to about twelve to fifteen men. Most of them knew as little, or even less, than I did about Jewish law, but we tried to do things right, to the best of our ability. We had some difficulty keeping track of the weekly *parshah*, though, and in a letter to Debby and Gil, I asked them to send me a Jewish calendar with the *sedrahs* for each week.

With time, I became more committed and began giving a great deal of thought to the services I led. I also became associated with several observant men during this period, most notably Chaplain Glenn (Moshe) Stengel.

Chaplain Stengel had joined the army after getting *smichah* from Yeshiva University in New York. He arrived in Vietnam two months after I did, in July 1968. Although he had first been scheduled to serve in a different area, he was sent to our region after his predecessor, Chaplain Singer, was killed in a plane crash. Chaplain Stengel was stationed in Phu Bai, which had been dubbed Rocket Alley by the soldiers because it was a favorite target of enemy fire.

As non-combatants, chaplains have a unique position in the military. They are not issued any weapons, only protective gear. Since they do not carry arms, a soldier is assigned to each chaplain to escort and protect him as he travels from base to base. Additionally, chaplains may be assigned to counsel men and women in several branches of the military during a single mission.

Chaplain Stengel is a man with a big heart and an enormous amount of energy. He worked tirelessly on behalf of the soldiers in his care, traveling constantly to meet with men of the Army, Navy, and Marines stationed throughout the region. He counseled, lifted spirits, and tried to organize gatherings to celebrate all the important Jewish dates.

In fact, the Chaplain's devotion extended to fallen soldiers too, and he sometimes visited the morgue to pray for those unfortunate young men who were about to be transported home. Indeed, the man in charge of one morgue remarked that Chaplain Stengel was the only chaplain he had ever seen step foot into the morgue.

Another man I got to know during this time was Navy Ensign Gary Siegel, who worked on the opposite end of the base in Da Nang. Siegel had grown up in a religious household and was able to lead the services very well. To my amazement, he could even *daven* without a *siddur*! I thought it was the most incredible thing I'd ever seen! The two of us began working together to arrange the weekly Shabbos services.

After a while, I observed one interesting difference between the Jewish congregation and the social gatherings of the non-Jews. When Jews gathered together, almost all of us were able to temporarily ignore military protocol. It didn't matter if one was a private or a colonel. As long as we were inside the chapel, there was no "Yes, sir" and "No, sir." We greeted each other with a friendly, "How ya' doin'?" and for a little while, we were just Jews praying together, pretty much on a first-name basis. This complete unity, regardless of rank, was rarely seen at the non-Jewish social gatherings I witnessed.

For Rosh Hashanah, Chaplain Stengel organized Jewish services in China Beach that was attended by over 300 Jewish soldiers who served in Vietnam. It was a powerful, moving experience, as so many Jews came together to pray in that remote location. Having taken a new interest in *Yiddishkeit*, it was a day of deep meaning and emotion for me, and the gathering left me charged with new, intensified spiritual energy.

One day, shortly after Rosh Hashanah, I met Lieutenant Colonel Daniel Pride in the mess hall in Da Nang. Pride was the battalion commander of the 63rd Maintenance Battalion in Quang Tri, Vietnam. Quang Tri was even farther north than Da Nang, just several miles south of the DMZ, which separated communist North Vietnam from South Vietnam. The Maintenance Battalion consisted of several units that worked to support the equipment and vehicles of other companies. They recovered and repaired tanks and jeeps and many other kinds of equipment that had been left in the field or had broken down. "Repair it or retrograde it" was their slogan.

As we conversed over breakfast, Colonel Pride mentioned that he was feeling very frustrated due to the many problems he was experiencing with some of his communications equipment.

"What's the problem, sir?" I asked.

"My communication equipment doesn't seem to be working properly," he said. "I have radios that work some of the time, and radios that hardly work at all. Frequently when I'm riding in my jeep and trying to reach headquarters here in Da Nang, I can't get through."

"Sir, I may be able to help you," I said eagerly. "I'm a Signal officer, and I am trained in communications. If I can take a look at the equipment, I may be able to figure out what's going on. In fact, I'm not very happy at my job here. Maybe I can join your unit and help out with all your communications needs."

"That would be great!" exclaimed the colonel. "Try to get authorization to come up to Quang Tri for several days, and if you see that this is, in fact, what you want to do, then I'll help you get approval for a transfer."

I had been getting more and more restless in my position and was thrilled at the thought of an imminent transfer. I quickly obtained permission from Major Stepp and soon found myself on a helicopter heading north toward Quang Tri Combat Base. I spent two days touring the base in a jeep and inspecting the communications equipment of the battalion. Unlike Da Nang, where I didn't usually wear my protective gear, I now kept my flak jacket and helmet on at all times. Since Quang Tri is closer to the DMZ, it was a much more dangerous area.

After examining several pieces of equipment and assessing the general situation, I had no trouble figuring out the problem. For anyone trained in communications, it was really a very simple matter.

There are two types of radio signals: AM (amplitude modulated) and FM (frequency modulated). AM radio signals travel around the earth's surface by bouncing off of the upper layers of the earth's atmosphere. AM signals can travel over extremely long distances—provided that high power transmitters are used. AM signals propagate in such a way that they are minimally affected by mountains and other topographic features.

FM, on the other hand, doesn't go around the curvature of the earth, but travels in a straight line. If there is any obstruction, like a mountain, for example, the transmission is lost. However, this is an advantage at times, since it makes the signal more secure. It travels like an arrow, heading directly towards the target, and doesn't scatter where enemy troops can tap into it and pick up the signal. Moreover, the FM signal is also a lot clearer to the listener and less affected by thunderstorms and other severe weather events.

During my inspection, I discovered that all the AM radios were working properly, and only the FM radios were problematic. Since there were mountains between Quang Tri and Da Nang, the FM signals were being interrupted, and it was no surprise that the messages weren't going through.

I solved the problem by arranging for the Army's Corps of Engineers to dig a deep hole in the ground. They then inserted a very tall telephone pole and placed antennas on top. Now, the signal could go straight up from the colonel's radio in his jeep to those antennas, and from there it was relayed straight over the mountains directly to Da Nang.

In addition to the radio problems, there were a number of other communication issues that had to be addressed. I looked forward to the challenge of tackling them all, and as soon as I returned to Da Nang, I took the necessary steps to obtain approval for my transfer. As I waited impatiently to join Lieutenant Colonel Pride and the 63rd Maintenance Battalion, I had no idea of what awaited me in Quang Tri. Solving the various communications equipment problems would by far be the least of my challenges.

0945 hrs
1 June, '69, Sunday
Da Nang

Dear Gil and Debby,

Thank you for your letters. They are wonderful!

I have received the wonderful news of your engagement and of your wedding plans, but I got your telegram about one month after you sent it.

... Gil, your letter I received yesterday. Thanks so much. ... How's the learning going? I've been attending (and actually helping out a little) with services here. Every week we get a few people together. Usually we just make a minion (sic) but sometimes only 6 or 7 can come. It's very difficult to take time off from work. ...

As it stands now, I work from 7 to 8 a.m. on Saturday, take from 8 to 11 off, and then work the rest of the day. ...

In Jerusalem now it must be beautiful. Shalom is the word for it. Shalom is not the word for this place, although someday I believe Vietnam may be one of the most beautiful places in the world. Its natural beauties are many, but today its people live like animals, except for those who have somehow managed to make money. Most of the people seem to be very poor, filthy, and undernourished. I saw much of the same situation when I was in South America.

I am sitting here at a wooden table now under a plastic roof writing to you. Helicopters fly every which way overhead. Occasionally a fast fighter zooms (or should I say 'screams') overhead. They travel at phenomenal speeds.

The U.S. Forces here are well-equipped. There is little question of that, but we seem to be falling down when it comes to communication of ideas to the lowest echelon. There are many soldiers here, and I must include high-ranking officers, who are here simply to put in their time and get out. They don't seem to have any true understanding of why we are fighting here. ...

The best of health and happiness to both of you forever. ... I hope to get [an engagement gift] in the mail to you soon. Happy Engagement!

Love, Hank

• • •

23 August, '69
1540 hrs
Saturday
Da Nang

Dear Mom,

Thanks for your letter dated 19 Aug. It was very moving, as your letters usually are. Your letters are a wonderful link between the real world and me. Don't stop.

... I am looking for a new job, however. Preferably one involving communications. I talked with the Corps Signal Officer in Phu Bai yesterday when I was there, and he gave me some encouragement.

... This morning I conducted services at the Air Force Chapel. We had 14 people show up. We had 15 last night! We're growing!

This morning we had probably the most unique Torah-reading service in the world. Here's a capsule version:

We open the ark and say the appropriate blessing. We carry the Torah around so that all may kiss it. We put the Torah back on the podium where it remains wrapped during the service. (None of the men present can read directly from the Torah.) We open the one Chumash we have and I call the first Aleah (sic). I read the first part of the Sedrah in Hebrew, but it takes so long that this is what happens:

Number 2 man blesses the portion.

Portion 2 I read in English.

The rest of the Sedrah I read in English.

What do you think? Pretty different, huh? I like it because so many of the congregants can't read Hebrew, let alone understand it; and I for one am certainly no expert.

One interesting thing, which Debby might be interested in, is this: The third or fourth Aleah happened to fall on a guy who knew his English name and his father's English name, but he didn't know the Hebrew names. Well, we figured out that Avraham would be the Hebrew equivalent for his English name, but no one knew how to say his father's name in Hebrew. After a little "conference", I just sang "Ya-Amode Avraham ben Yisroel"... (Well, Debby, did I do OK?)

Yesterday, as I said, I went to Phu Bai. The trip was really an excuse for me to get out of the office and take a Spec 5 with me who has been doing outstanding work for me and everyone else around here for a long time. We boarded a Huey at 1100 and flew between 200 and 500 feet altitude (very low) over the beach line until we neared the Hai Van Pass. (Take a look at the map. It's about halfway between here and Phu Bai.) At that point we increased our altitude considerably and whizzed over the pass. The pass is a favorite area for "Charlie" to fire at us from. Fortunately, there were no incidents either on the way up or the way back. (Frankly, flying over the pass is no more dangerous, in my opinion, than driving around Da Nang to services on Friday night. I'm not saying this just to put you at ease, but so that you can gain some perspective of the situation. You see, driving through Da

Nang at night is generally considered asking for problems, as is flying at night. …

Well, I've stolen enough time from my work. …

I trust and pray that all at home are fine and healthy. I'm healthy and manage to smile often. Keep up your faith that soon the nations of the world will beat their swords into plowshares. Until we can rest with some real assurance of that being a reality, however, keep supporting the troops here. We all need to know that people at home appreciate the efforts being made to keep the NVA and VC from harassing villages and torturing people and bringing the disgusting realities of Communism as I have seen it practiced to this country. The setup the South Vietnamese have now may be far from ideal, but at least there is an army to protect the system, to enforce the laws, and to defend the people against attackers. Most of the trouble-makers are in small groups in the hills and come out to fight at night in squads or companies. They harass. They snipe. They lay mines, blow up bridges, and treat human beings as animals. I don't know these people well, but I do believe the US Govt is trying to do something constructive here. Sometimes I also believe many of the administrators of the forces here don't have a clear idea of how they want to accomplish that. Sometimes I believe they are afraid to think logically and openly. Sometimes I don't know what to think.

One thing I know. Only 200 some odd days to go. Everyone counts here.

I love you all. Stay well. …

ILY,

Hank

19 September, '69
1000 hrs
Da Nang

Dear Gil,

First let me wish both you and Deb the very best of health and happiness for the New Year. You both deserve the very best.

Next, thank you for the calendar. It arrived a few moments ago, via Deb and my father. Dad suggested that maybe you didn't have my address, and that's why you sent the calendar through Debby. ...

How's the yeshiva? We have a Rabbi here ... who graduated from the Yeshiva University in New York. I guess there's a lot of difference between his yeshiva and yours, though.

Our Rosh Hashanah services were good. We had over 300 men (and one woman) participate. Tonight I lead services at the Air Force Chapel and Rabbi Stengel (the guy from Phu Bai who attended the N.Y. Yeshiva) will be our guest. ...

Well, I must go now. My most recent reports from Waltham indicate that Debby and all the Webbs are fine. ...

I am moving to a new and more challenging assignment in 7 days. It will be in a place called Quang Tri... My address will be:

Me
Signal Equipment Maintenance Officer
63rd Maintenance BN
26th General Support Group
Quang Tri, Vietnam

CHAPTER SIX

EXCITEMENT AT QUANG TRI

On September 26, 1969, I finally left Da Nang for good. I arrived at Quang Tri Combat Base carrying all my personal belongings, including every soldier's most valuable possession, my "short timer's calendar." Whether it hung next to his bed or on the door of his locker, *everyone* in Vietnam had a short timer's calendar *somewhere*. The short timer's calendar consisted of the months or weeks that were left of the soldier's service in Vietnam. Every day was dutifully crossed off, so that the soldier could keep an exact count of how many months, weeks, and days remained. In fact, some soldiers even kept track of the hours and minutes!

A year or two before I came to Quang Tri, the place was a hotbed of activity. By the time I arrived, things had calmed down considerably, but the attacks were still more frequent here than in Da Nang. We always had to be on the alert, because the attacks could begin again at any time. Sometimes, however, there would be peace and quiet for weeks.

The base in Quang Tri was very primitive. Some soldiers poured buckets of water over each other to "shower." Later, makeshift wooden structures were built with a number of small shower stalls that provided the luxury of a true shower, albeit still with ice-cold water.

In Quang Tri, I became both the Battalion Signal Officer *and* the Signal Equipment Maintenance Officer. I was responsible for everything from field phones to counter-mortar radars. I had to ensure that everything was installed and working properly.

When I first arrived, there were several major problems that had to be addressed. In addition, some new communications equipment had to be installed. However, after several hectic weeks, things calmed down a bit.

As part of my duties, I was also adjutant (glorified secretary) to the Battalion Commander, and I had my own office in the headquarters building. A newspaper was published there for the men fighting in the area, and I put in a little announcement that Sabbath services would be held Friday night and Saturday morning in the battalion chapel. As in Da Nang, a handful of people came at first, but soon their numbers increased.

Although I didn't know much, I soon became the self-appointed Jewish lay leader on the DMZ. The place lacked Jewish books and supplies, though, and I wrote my father, telling him of our situation. My father contacted the National Jewish Welfare Board in New York, and a short time later

I received a box that was filled with *tallaisim, yarmulkes, siddurim*, and other much-needed materials. The package was accompanied by a warm letter that was written by a woman named Eiga Hershman. She recommended that I contact the Jewish chaplain, Chaplain Glenn Stengel, whom I had already met, to help me.

I followed her suggestion and invited Chaplain Stengel to come spend a Shabbos in Quang Tri. I wanted him to lead the Shabbos services and give me advice on how to bring some more *Yiddishkeit* to the base.

Chaplain Stengel was brought to us by a Special Forces helicopter from Phu Bai on a Friday afternoon. Shortly before his arrival, we received intelligence reports warning us of plans for an imminent enemy attack on our base. Therefore, on Friday night, I slept in my boots and flak jacket and kept my loaded weapon handy next to my bed.

Unfortunately, the report proved to be accurate. At about 0300 hours (three o'clock in the morning), we were awakened by the shrill whistle of incoming rockets. After several seconds, there was an earsplitting explosion. The sky lit up as the rockets continued coming in, one after another. Soon we could discern the sound of our own artillery and nearby machine guns returning fire. The place was in an uproar.

We all jumped out of bed, preparing to run towards our assigned battle positions. One fellow, Captain Doug McGill, also slept in my hooch. He was an extraordinary man, and I consider him one of the *chasidei umos haolam*.

"Here," McGill said, holding out his flak jacket to Chaplain Stengel. "Take this. You will probably be needed down at the battalion headquarters bunker to assist the dying with their spiritual needs."

I looked at my friend incredulously. I could not believe that he was ready to go into battle without his flak jacket for protection! I wasn't about to part from mine, and here he was offering to give his away to a Jewish chaplain whom he barely knew. It was truly amazing! After handing the jacket to Chaplain Stengel, he ran out, completely exposed, to do his job.

I followed Doug into the night, running toward the sector for which I was responsible. The noise was incredible, and the entire sky was illuminated, so that I had no trouble seeing where I was going.

In addition to one's regular duties, everyone on base also had a designated position that he had to assume in the event of an attack. I was in charge of defending one section of the perimeter, which included nine bunkers that were each manned by four or five soldiers. The "bunkers" were not dug into the ground, but they were small areas that were enclosed with sandbags for protection.

I was in constant communication with the men I commanded, directing their fire toward the enemy's position. After some time, I suddenly lost communication with some of the bunkers. It was imperative that I be in contact with my men at all times. I was now forced into the terrible position of having to order one of my men into a life-threatening situation. Luckily, one young soldier, Sergeant Bob Emery, instantly agreed to crawl toward the perimeter and try to restore communication.

As Emery slithered away through the mud, I highly doubted that I would ever see the man alive again. There were

Back row from left: Debby, Sally, Marc, and me.
Front from left: Mom, Heidi, Sam, and Dad.

On the Charles River off our backyard, 1965.

▲*Above:* With Uncle Julius, in Revolutionary-era uniform, during a visit to Lexington.

◄*Left:* With my bass fiddle

Repairing my bass fiddle with my father.

Playing my guitar during one of our family camping trips.

▲*Above:* Dad and Sam filling our "washing machine."

▶*Right:* Me on one of our hikes.

Climbing the breathtaking Worthington Glacier in Alaska on July 12, 1962. Richardson Highway en route to Valdez.

Celebrating a birthday in front of our camper. *Left to right:* Me, Sally, Marc, Dad, Mom, Debby. *Front:* Heidi and Sam.

◄ *Left:* Army photo taken around 1967.

▼ *Below:* The Signal Corps insignia that is pinned to the lapel of my uniform.

Da Nang city.

My first hooch. May, 1969.

Chaplain Stengel during High Holidays, 1969. *(Army photo)*

Lighting the menorah in Quang Tri. Chanukah, 1969. *(I'm not sure why I'm wearing a talis here. I must have assumed that since it's worn during prayers, I must don it for any religious ceremony.)*

Some of the letters that appear in this book:

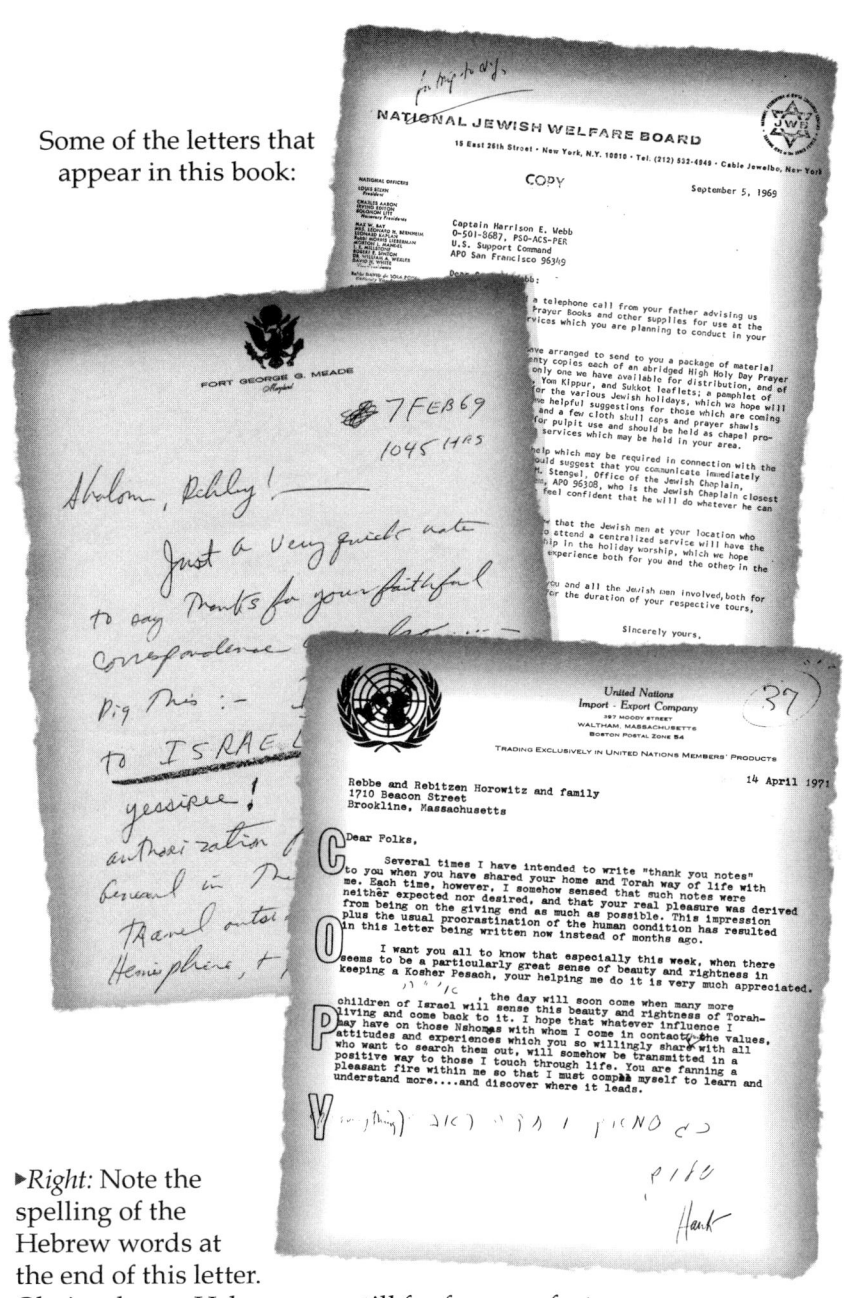

▶ *Right:* Note the spelling of the Hebrew words at the end of this letter. Obviously, my Hebrew was still far from perfect.

Excitement At Quang Tri

Here I'm inspecting a truck during Reserve Training in Fort Lee, Virginia. July 21, 1971. *(Army photo by PFC M. Keller)*

Proudly wearing my yarmulke as I *bentch* in the mess in Fort Lee. *(Army photo by PFC M. Keller)*

▲ *Above:* "Flying high" in the pilot's seat.

◄ *Left:* My father putting on *tefillin* with a *shaliach* in Brazil.

▼ *Below:* Receiving *kos shel bracha* from the Rebbe. My sons, Eitan and Avi, are behind me.

◀ *Left:* My wife and I at the wedding of Sender and Chami, June 2002.

▼ *Below:* At the chasunah of our son, Asher. Adar 5764, February 2004. Back row from left: Rochel, Chami holding Rivka, Doba, Asher, Avi, Sender, Loozy. Middle: Gitty, my mother, Gertrude, my wife, Chaya, myself, Eitan holding Leibel. Front: Mushka, Ahuva, Simcha.

bullets flying everywhere, and it was unlikely that he would manage to avoid them all. Nonetheless, the sergeant bravely did his job. He followed the wire and, incredibly, managed to repair it while the firefight raged around him. I believed I was witnessing a miracle when I saw him crawl back unscathed shortly thereafter. I was immensely relieved to see him back alive.

The battle continued uninterrupted for two hours. About halfway through, I could no longer command effectively, since I was unable to see what was going on outside my bunker. There was an observation tower with four soldiers inside directly above the bunker where I sat huddled with several men. I decided to go up there to get a better view of the enemy's position.

While the tower itself was fortified against enemy fire, I was exposed during my climb up the ladder. I tried to ascend as quickly as possible, despite the heavy protective equipment that I was wearing and the rifle slung over my shoulder. Just as I was standing on the top rung, about to step over the tower's railing, a bullet came straight towards me. I felt a breeze as it whizzed by, grazing my right ear as it passed. I hurled myself over the railing, startling the four guys who were crouching inside as I fell on top of them.

As I lay on my back, looking up at a sky ablaze, I wondered whether I was still alive. Was this what death felt like? I had *heard* the bullet; I had *felt* its breeze. Was it possible that my life wasn't over yet?

I pinched myself hard. Surprisingly, it hurt. An odd sensation came over me, as I listened to the sound of my breathing in disbelief. I had never felt more alive, as I suddenly became keenly aware of each intake of breath.

At that moment, I was overcome with a tremendous sense of gratitude to Hashem. "Thank you, G-d," I whispered. "You kept me alive. Please help me get through this until the end. I know that you saved me for a purpose. I must have something important to do with my life. I will try my best to figure out what that is, and I will do whatever You want of me. Just keep me alive and give me a chance to fulfill this promise."

All this happened in a matter of seconds, but it was a moment of truth and incredible inspiration. I quickly got to my feet and surveyed the battlefield. I saw incoming fire that originated from an enemy position on the right side of the perimeter. I directed my men to aim toward that position, and I fired at it as well. Soon the firing from that location ceased. I will never know if my bullets killed or injured anyone, but I do know that we all fired in self-defense.

At about 0500 hours, just as the first rays of sunlight appeared, the incoming fire stopped completely. The long, terrible night was finally over.

As I climbed down from the observation tower and inspected the surrounding area, I found a young man who had been hit in the stomach. I stopped a sergeant who was driving a jeep nearby. Together, we dragged the man onto the front seat, placing him between us. While the driver made his way toward the hospital tent, the young soldier was losing color in his face with each passing moment. He was bleeding profusely, and I literally had to hold his stomach together with my hands. At last, we reached the surgical area, where doctors began treating him immediately. (The man lived for several days, and

I stopped by twice to visit him. Sadly, he died while he was being transferred by air to a hospital in Japan.)

As I headed out of the hospital tent, I saw several doctors trying to revive a Montagnyard Vietnamese girl. With all the wounded soldiers coming in, they were short in staff, and I offered to hold up a bottle of solution for them.

The girl, who was about fourteen years old, was terribly malnourished and weighed only about fifty pounds. Her heart had stopped beating, but the doctors managed to get it working again. It was a short-lived victory, though, as only a couple of minutes later, her heart stopped once more. The doctors tried various extreme procedures, but this time, with no success. Eventually, the young girl died on table. The doctors had tried their best, and although I was very traumatized by the incident, it was a good feeling to know that our troops were willing to do their utmost to help local nationals with medical emergencies, as well as our own soldiers. When I finally walked out, I was in a daze and barely managed to make it back to my hooch.

By now, I could no longer ignore the deep yearning I felt in my heart for a more committed lifestyle. Like the trip to Israel, my sudden brush with death was a major turning point, and it made me long for a more meaningful life. Thus, shortly after the terrible battle, I decided to begin observing the Shabbos. I was trying to make good on my commitment to Hashem that "I will do whatever You want of me."

Although I didn't know much about keeping Shabbos, I did know some basic rules that I had managed to pick up. I knew, for example, that writing, traveling, and talking on the phone were all forbidden. This provided some challenges, since my job at the headquarters office required me to do quite a bit of writing.

Generally, the men on base were given the day off on Sunday. They would go out to a nearby beach, grill hamburgers and play volleyball. I decided to request that I be given the day off on Saturday instead of Sunday. Of course, in the case of a firefight, or other military emergency, I would join the other men in the field, but at least when things were peaceful, I would be able to rest on Shabbos.

With this plan in mind, I approached my boss, Lieutenant Colonel Pride, nervously. Although he was a nice man and we got along well, he had no tolerance for someone who, he believed, was trying to "shirk duty." He was not interested in excuses and was outraged when he observed laziness in his men.

"Sir," I began, "I would like to make a request. I know that we all get a day off on Sunday, but for me, I'm Jewish … and Saturday is our day of rest. I want to take off on Saturdays, so that I can help with the Jewish services and avoid doing work, like writing, in the office. I will make up for it by working on Sundays instead.

"And of course, sir," I added quickly, "it is self-understood that in case of an attack on Saturday, you can be sure that I will be the first one in the field to help defend my sector of the perimeter."

Pride looked at me with an amused smile. "Webb," he said in his deep Southern drawl, "I had a Jew-boy neighbor who lived next door, and he was Orthodox, mind you. Every Saturday, the two of us would mow the lawn together. So I figure, if that

Orthodox Jew-boy could mow the lawn on Saturday, there's no reason why you can't come in and push a pencil on Saturday."

For a moment, I was speechless. How could I explain that his "Orthodox" neighbor was clearly not? However, I was not ready to give in. Before coming to speak to the colonel, I had done some research, and I had come across an army regulation stating that "All Sabbath observing personnel shall be given time off, consistent with military exigencies."

Knowing my rights as a soldier, I proceeded to make the biggest mistake of my career and blurted out: "Sir, with all due respect to your rank, I think there's a higher authority than you."

No sooner had the words left my mouth, then the colonel's face turned red with rage. I had spoken disrespectfully. This was considered an insult and "insubordination" to a superior officer. The man was livid!

"Webb," he said in a barely controlled voice, as he gritted his teeth in anger, "the general will hear about this."

I trembled as I left his presence, as visions of a court martial and dishonorable discharge flashed through my mind. I could be thrown into jail, I realized. This could be the end of my military career.

My emotions were in turmoil as I prayed with the other men that Friday night. After services, I went directly to my hooch and soon fell into a restless sleep.

When I woke up on Shabbos morning, I had to make one of the most important decisions of my life. I could go to work as usual, or I could risk a court martial for "disobeying a lawful order of a superior officer"—in a time of war! I felt that I was standing at a crossroads, and I didn't know which road to take. True, it was a time of war. But even so, there had been a lull for weeks, except for one major firefight. It was really a time of relative peace and quiet.

In the end, I resolutely decided to observe this Shabbos, come what may. At the time, I couldn't say from where that incredible resolve stemmed. In retrospect, I believe Hashem gave me the special strength I needed. I became determined to stand firm and not yield to the wishes of the colonel.

"I came here to fight for freedom," I thought to myself, "including the freedom of religion. Well, I have rights, too, and shouldn't I be able to practice my own religion? If not, then what am I putting my life at risk for?"

A sense of peace washed over me, and I calmly walked to Shabbos morning services. As soon as the prayers were over, I decided to make myself scarce. I was in no mood for a confrontation, so I wanted to avoid any place where I might encounter Colonel Pride.

The base covered a very large area, and I began circling around the perimeter, away from where the barracks and buildings were situated. The grass at the edge of the perimeter was very high, even taller than a human being, and there I could walk undisturbed, hidden from view. Many booby traps and mines had been placed there to prevent the Viet Cong from entering the base. I had spent lots of time in the sector that I had to defend during enemy attacks, so I knew the precise areas where the traps had been laid. For someone who was not familiar with the area, it could be suicidal to walk around there. But since I knew the "safe" areas, it was the ideal place for me to hide. No one would dream of looking for me there.

After strolling around for a while, I took a Soncino Chumash from the battalion chapel and went deep into the tall grass. No one could see me; I was safe. It was incredibly hot. I took off my shirt and stretched out on the ground. I opened the *Chumash* and began reading the English translation of the week's *parshah*. Suddenly, I came across a verse that shocked me to the core: "*Sheishes yamim ta'avod v'asisah kal melachtechah v'yom hashvieie shabbos l'Hashem...*: Six days shalt thou labor and do all thy work, but the seventh day is a Sabbath onto the Lord thy G-d."

I could not believe my eyes. What incredible *hashgachah* that, of the entire Torah, this should be the *posuk* that I found!

I read the verse again and clapped my hands with joy. "There *is* a Higher Authority," I exclaimed with excitement. Earlier, I had referred to the army regulation as the higher authority, but now, right before my eyes, I read Hashem's commandment to His Chosen People: "… the seventh day is a Sabbath onto the Lord thy G-d."

It now became clear to me, more than ever, Who was *really* running the show. Forget Colonel Pride and the general! Hashem was in command! This deep awareness took my breath away and made me feel confident that I had made the right choice.

Suddenly, I recalled an incident of my youth. I was sitting beside my father in the front seat of the car during a heavy downpour. It seemed as though the skies had opened, allowing buckets of water to gush down. As my father drove down the street, he suddenly spotted our rabbi, Rabbi Aaron Kra. He was getting drenched to the bone as he walked through the rain. It was Friday night, and we knew that the Rabbi didn't drive on Shabbos.

My father pulled up next to him and rolled down his window. "Hey, you want a lift, Rabbi?" he asked.

"No, thank you," Rabbi Kra replied. "Good Shabbos."

"Oh, come on, you're dripping wet. Please, get into the car."

Rabbi Kra simply shook his head. "No, it's okay. Don't worry about it. It's a matter of principle."

I could not help but admire the man. He had not even considered my father's offer for a moment. I was amazed at his commitment to his faith and his willingness to put himself in such an unpleasant situation to avoid violating the laws of Shabbos.

Now, I could suddenly identify with Rabbi Kra. For me, it wasn't just a matter of getting wet. I had truly put my military career on the line on account of my beliefs. And the *Chumash* had assured me that I had acted correctly. Hashem was on *my* side. And while I hoped to remain a loyal soldier in the U.S. Armed Forces, I was also determined to remain faithful to the true Commander-in-Chief.

For the moment, there appeared to be no way to honor my obligations to one without appearing disloyal to the other, but after the incredible revelation I had just experienced, I was no longer concerned. A sense of tranquility enveloped me as my duty suddenly became crystal clear: I had to do my best to behave as a true, loyal soldier. Somehow, I believed, everything else would fall into place. My Commander would see to that.

In the late afternoon, I finally began heading back to my hooch. I felt euphoric, as though I had just made some incredible, life-altering discovery. Nonetheless, I was not ready to face the colonel quite yet. I knew that he was mad at me and I wanted to stay out of his sight.

Trying to keep a low profile, I went quietly to bed and soon fell asleep. On Sunday morning, just as I was getting dressed, I suddenly heard my name on the loudspeaker. "Captain Webb, Captain Webb. Report immediately to battalion Headquarters. This is an emergency!"

I jumped up and ran for the door. Although I had my M16 rifle in my wall locker nearby, I was so startled by the unexpected announcement that I left it behind. I also had no time to strap my .45 caliber pistol around my waist. As I ran out of my hooch, I couldn't help wondering why I had been summoned if, as the announcer said, there was indeed an emergency. Why hadn't they called Colonel Pride or one of the other superior officers?

As I neared the building, it quickly became apparent that something unusual was indeed happening. About fifty or sixty men who worked in the building were standing anxiously outside.

"What's going on?" I asked breathlessly when I arrived at the scene.

"There's a soldier inside with a hand grenade!" I was told. "He's threatening to blow up the place. We all ran out, but he's still in there."

It was a dangerous situation, as I realized that if he were indeed to use the grenade, we could all be hurt or killed.

At this moment, I became acutely aware of the fact that I had run out of my hooch empty-handed. "Hey," I said to a soldier standing next to me, "let me borrow your weapon!"

"No, sir. It's mine," he replied.

In truth, the man was not trying to be disrespectful. In the army, every soldier is responsible for his or her own weapon. No one is ever obligated to part from his weapon—not even when a superior officer demands it. I could not expect someone to give up his rifle and put himself in possible jeopardy just because I had failed to bring my own.

I had no choice but to enter the building unarmed. In retrospect, I realize that it was Hashem's guiding hand that led me to leave my rifle behind. Who knows how the panic-stricken soldier would have reacted at the sight of a captain barging in with a weapon in his hands? He might have thrown the grenade the instant he saw me.

"Okay, I'm going in," I announced.

So, with no weapon to protect me, I walked into the building. I immediately spotted a young black private at the far end of a long hallway. He just stood there, holding something in his hand.

Despite my fear, I assumed an air of calmness and confidence. "Soldier, I'm not going to hurt you," I said soothingly. "Don't worry. No one's going to hurt you. Relax. I just want to talk with you."

I walked steadily down the hallway, maintaining constant eye contact with him. When I was standing within arm's reach, I asked in the same even tone of voice, "What's going on? What do you have in your hand?"

He looked at me hesitantly and then, as I slowly stretched my empty hands towards him, he dropped the grenade into the palm of my hand. Fortunately, the pin had not yet been pulled, so the timing mechanism inside was not activated. I closed my fingers tightly around it and looked up. The soldier's eyes were open wide in fear.

I put my hand gently on his shoulder, steered him into Colonel Pride's office, and sat him into the big chair behind the colonel's desk. "How about a cup of coffee?" I asked amiably.

The terrified soldier nodded meekly. I walked over to the coffee machine in the corner and poured some into a cup. I handed it to him.

"You don't have to tell me anything," I said, as he began sipping the coffee. "Whatever you say can be used against you in a court of law. But you must give me your name, rank, and serial number."

He quietly gave me the information, and I quickly jotted it down on a piece of paper. Then, as he continued sipping from his cup, I walked a few steps to the front door with the grenade and gave the anxious crowd the all-clear signal.

At that very moment, as I lifted my arm to the men in the yard, Major Carl Van Sickle, my superior officer, arrived from R&R in Tokyo. He watched in bewilderment as the soldiers began cheering excitedly when I appeared at the front door of the building.

I went back inside while the others explained the situation to him. Within several minutes, the Military Police arrived. They arrested the soldier and took a detailed report from me.

From the MP's, I learned the story behind the unusual turn of events. That morning, the private had gone to the Post Exchange, the commerce area on the base, where various merchandise is sold. He admired a wristwatch that was on display, and as he walked out with it, the Vietnamese girl behind the counter asked him to pay.

"But I already paid!" the private insisted.

An argument ensued and the Military Police were called. They arrested him and took him down to the police bunker. Claiming innocence, the young man was furious, and he yelled and cursed at the police in anger. In the confusion, there were apparently a few moments when he was not properly guarded. He somehow managed to get hold of a grenade in the MP bunker. Holding it in his hand, he escaped and then ran up the street to our battalion Headquarters.

But why was I the one to be called? After further investigation, the puzzle pieces started to fall into place.

The general, who was supposed to visit our unit, was detained and never showed up. Colonel Pride had been called away to attend to some matter. Major Carl Van Sickle was in Tokyo on R&R. Thus, through incredible *hashgachah pratis*, all those outranking me were missing, and I was the senior captain and had become Acting Battalion Commander by default. Unarmed, I had confronted a disturbed, grenade-wielding private, and I had managed to diffuse the situation without causing injury to myself or other soldiers, or damage to the Headquarters building. I was the talk of the unit.

After this event, I no longer had any problem with observing Shabbos. I sensed that Major Van Sickle and others on the base viewed me as a hero. Colonel Pride, the man who had threatened to report me, said nothing at all. He never praised my actions, nor did he mention anything about Shabbos. The entire matter became a non-issue. He simply looked the other way and allowed me to do as I pleased without interference. I was able to continue spending time leading Shabbos services in the battalion chapel on Shabbos morning, and during the day, I either roamed around the base or went into my office to speak with my subordinates. I didn't write; I didn't travel in any vehicles; and I didn't use the phone. And, as promised, I came in to work every Sunday.

The men who worked for me at the adjutant's office wanted to send a report to higher headquarters, recommending that I receive a special medal for bravery. I discouraged them, though, insisting that I had just been doing my duty. Besides, with Shabbos observance no longer an issue, I felt that I had already been rewarded. My revelation on the day before the incident had been reinforced. Hashem was in control, and He was taking care of me.

NATIONAL JEWISH WELFARE BOARD

15 East 26th Street, New York, NY 10010 Tel: (212) 532-4949

September 5, 1969

Captain Harrison E. Webb
0-501-8687, PSO-ACS-PER
U.S. Support Command
APO San Francisco 96349

Dear Captain Webb:

    We have received a telephone call from your father advising us of your need for Prayer Books and other supplies for use at the High Holy Day Services which you are planning to conduct in your area.

    In response, we have arranged to send to you a package of material which includes twenty copies each of an abridged High Holy Day Prayer Book, which is the only one we have available for distribution, and of our Rosh Hashanah, Yom Kippur, and Sukkot leaflets; a pamphlet of sermonic material for the various Jewish holidays, which we hope will provide some helpful suggestions for those which are coming up on the calendar; and a few cloth skull caps and prayer shawls which are intended for pulpit use and should be held as chapel property for any future services which may be held in your area.

For any additional help which may be required in connection with the High Holy Days, we would suggest that you communicate immediately with Chaplain Glenn M. Stengel, Office of the Jewish Chaplain, Hq XXIV Corps, Vietnam, APO 96308, who is the Jewish Chaplain closest to your location. We feel confident that he will do whatever he can to be helpful to you.

It is gratifying to know that the Jewish men at your location who are not in a position to attend centralized service will have the benefit of your leadership in the holiday worship, which we hope will prove an enriching experience both for you and the others in the congregation.

With every good wish to you and all the Jewish men involved, both for the coming New Year and for the duration of your respective tours,

Sincerely yours,
(Miss) Eiga Hershman
Administrative Assistant

CHAPTER SEVEN
Never A Dull Moment

As things quieted down in Quang Tri, I once again settled into the old, familiar routine. Wake up at 0600 hours. Eat breakfast of eggs, salad, and bread in the mess hall. Attend the daily morning meeting of the headquarters staff. And of course, continue crossing off days from my ever-shrinking "short timer's calendar."

At around this time, I wanted to begin keeping kosher, in addition to my Shabbos observance. The only *kashrus* rule that I was aware of at this point was the prohibition of mixing meat and dairy. Thus, I stopped eating cheeseburgers and partaking of meat and dairy at the same meal.

While things were once more peaceful on the base, there were two men in Quang Tri who were determined to make my life miserable. Captain Charlie Jones and his sidekick, First Lieutenant Williams, were both Jew-hating Southern villains who loved to go out of their way to cause me trouble. From the day they discovered that I was Jewish, they couldn't walk past me without muttering some curse or insult.

One day I was doing some work in the retrograde yard, where obsolete and broken down trucks and tanks were disposed of. I was about to walk back to the battalion Headquarters, which was at the other end of the base, when Williams came down in a jeep. "Hey, can I have a ride back with you?" I called.

"You - - - ing Jew!" he yelled, adding a string of other obscenities for good measure. "I wouldn't help you Jews with anything!"

I was shocked and outraged by his reply. Not only was I offended by his words, but such insolent behavior toward someone of higher rank is totally unacceptable in the army! He deserved to be court-martialed for disrespect to a superior officer!

As he sped away, leaving a trail of dust behind him, I was so enraged that my heart began pounding violently. After I finally got back to my office, I immediately sat down to write up a report of his intolerable, rude behavior. Somehow, as I vented my rage with my pen, it seemed to transfer from my chest onto the piece of paper. By the time I was done, my anger had cooled off. I began questioning the wisdom of submitting the report and decided against taking any immediate action. In the end, it remained in my drawer and, as I became busy with other pressing matters, I simply put it out of my mind.

Perhaps this incident should have warned me that worse was still to come.

One evening, I was sitting in the Officers' Club with my good friend Captain Doug McGill and some other officers. The Officers' Club was a place where we could hang out and relax at the end of a hard day's work. The main attraction there, of course, was the beer that was sold at the bar, but one could also buy hamburgers, hotdogs, and other refreshments. For additional entertainment, officers could play at one of the gambling machines that had been installed in the club.

(Incidentally, I once put a quarter into one of those "one-armed bandits" and won the jackpot, which I think was about $25. A big guy was standing next to me when it happened, and he exclaimed, "Hey! Them's my quarters!" He was completely serious, too! Since he'd been dropping quarters into the machine all night long, he felt it was unfair that I came along, put in one quarter, and won all "his" money. Wanting to avoid a major brawl, I offered to give him half of the proceeds, and he was happy.)

As I was conversing with my friends at a table in the corner, Captain Charlie Jones sauntered into the room. Jones was a large, muscular fellow, and it was easy to be intimidated by him. As he glanced around the room, his eyes fell upon me and his face twisted in revulsion.

Perhaps the man had gulped down one drink too many. I will never know what prompted his sudden display of hatred and anger. "You! You dirty Jew!" he fumed. "I wouldn't even let you into my state!"

I stood up and made some response, and suddenly Jones completely lost whatever self-control he had previously possessed. He began cursing and screaming, yelling one insult after another. Suddenly, he reached for his weapon. Things seemed to move in slow motion as my eyes opened wide in terror and disbelief. I was paralyzed with fear. It was obvious that the man was not simply trying to intimidate me. He was set on killing me!

At that moment, McGill jumped to his feet and placed himself between us. "Webb didn't do anything to you!" he yelled to Jones. He put his two hands on the bigger man's chest and pushed him toward the door. "Get out of here! Now!" he roared.

Captain Jones stormed out the door. I fell into a chair in shock, too traumatized to move or speak. I whispered some words of gratitude to McGill for his incredible bravery. The man had, quite simply, saved my life.

Although there weren't many cases of homicide on the base, there were some rare exceptions. At one time, there was a sergeant who was despised by some of his men. I never learned whether this deep loathing was caused by mistreatment and harassment or some other obnoxious behavior. Whatever the case, someone placed a grenade under his bunk, and it exploded during the night. The man was killed instantly. To my knowledge, the culprit was never found or brought to justice.

During my encounter with Captain Jones, I never had any doubt about his intention to kill me. It is quite clear that without the interference of Captain McGill, he would have gone ahead with the act. He was in such a state at the time, that I don't think he even once considered—or cared about—the consequences he would have to face later.

After the incident, I thought about sending a report to Headquarters. In the end, I decided against it, because I was afraid I would just make matters worse. I would have to bring up the anti-Semitic motivations, and I sensed that I might not find sympathetic ears. Unfortunately, unlike law and order in civilian life, in a war zone, it's the "law of the jungle" that sometimes prevails. If someone submits a negative report on a fellow soldier and that person has friends who are more powerful, the action could backfire, and the accuser could be the one in trouble. In many instances, to avoid further aggravation, it seemed best to look the other way.

As a Jew, I knew this was especially true for me. I realized that Jones might have some like-minded, high-ranking friends, who would make sure to avenge my actions on his behalf.

Luckily, I was soon able to take some time off. I received word of an upcoming conference of Jewish chaplains serving on the Asian continent and in surrounding areas. It was scheduled to take place in Tokyo, and, although I wasn't a chaplain, I decided to attend, as the self-appointed Jewish lay leader on the DMZ.

I obtained authorization to leave on R&R on the appropriate date. When I arrived at the hotel in Toyko, I received a royal welcome, as I was the only person from Vietnam at the convention. Unlike me, the others had come from relatively peaceful areas, and they seemed to be awed to have in their midst someone who had come directly from the war zone. Thus, even though I wasn't officially a chaplain, they went out of their way to make me feel at ease.

There were about twenty Jewish chaplains in all at the conference. We spent a wonderful Shabbos together, giving each other *chizuk* and discussing ways to bring more *Yiddishkeit* to the Jewish soldiers who were serving so far away from home.

All too soon it was time to head back to Quang Tri. Although I wished I could spend more time with the Jewish chaplains, the gathering had rejuvenated me, and I returned to the base in high spirits.

To my good fortune, a second R&R opportunity presented itself as well. A friend who made the traveling arrangements for soldiers taking R&R informed me that there was one extra seat on a flight taking soldiers to Australia. "If you want it, you can have it," he told me. "Otherwise, it will be wasted."

I requested authorization to take a second R&R for one week to Sydney, Australia, and permission was granted.

At this time, I already had my pilot's license and was eager to fly again. I wanted to obtain an international pilot's license, or at least an Australian one, too. That way, I dreamed, I would be better equipped to do international business once I left the military.

While in Sydney, I met Rabbi Feldman and his family, *shluchim* of the Lubavitcher Rebbe, and spent some time with them. I also took a flying test at Sydney's main airport and received a temporary flying permit. After some persuasion, I convinced Rabbi Feldman to take a short ride over the airfield with me. It was exhilarating to be piloting a plane once again, and after the trip, I returned to my post in Quang Tri in high spirits.

Though all soldiers looked forward to their R&R, these short getaways were certainly not enough to help us cope with the many tribulations of war. To the soldier, a sense of humor is as essential for survival as any weapon. Not surprisingly, the men on base loved to play pranks and tell tall tales, and of course, any incident that drew laughs was enthusiastically repeated by soldiers in mess halls and on the field.

One such story that circulated during my time in Quang Tri involved an armored unit located nearby. An officer was scheduled to visit their base for an inspection, to determine whether the number of equipment and personnel matched those of the army records.

Unfortunately, like other bureaucratic government agencies, the army has some senseless, time-consuming regulations and endless red tape, which often lead to mismanagement and failed communication. Predictably, the number of equipment recorded on file does not always match the amount that is actually in the field.

Shortly before the inspection, the men of the armored unit realized that they had one more tank than was listed in their official records. No one knew how this came to be. The soldiers panicked as they realized that they would be subjected to the inspector's cross-examination, as he would try to determine how the army could lose track of such a costly, monstrous vehicle.

In desperation, the men came up with an ingenious solution. They dug a wide ditch in the corner of the base and drove one of their tanks into it. They then camouflaged it with some leaves and bushes until there was no trace of the oversized vehicle.

Later, when the army inspector arrived, the men proudly escorted him through the base, and he noted with satisfaction that the number of tanks in the field matched perfectly with the number in his records. Of course, he never could have guessed that another tank was hidden away nearby, several feet in the ground!

In a similar incident, another unit was short one jeep when they were up for inspection. When the soldiers turned to a neighboring unit for assistance, the men agreed to lend one of their jeeps for the duration of the inspection on condition that they would be "compensated" for their actions. Thus, a pallet containing dozens of cases of beer was promptly delivered. While the men tore apart the cases and eagerly emptied the bottles, their friends drove off in one of their jeeps and managed to pass their inspection without incident.

We all laughed appreciatively at these and other stories. For a little while, we could forget the death and horror around us and relieve some of our anxiety with a hearty belly laugh. Humor always boosted morale and helped the days go by faster.

Soon, my service in Vietnam was drawing to a close. My "short timer's calendar" consisted of only a couple of weeks. With great excitement, I began looking forward to returning home and finally seeing my family and friends again.

Images of happy reunions now danced before my eyes each night. Although I didn't think of myself as a hero, I was hoping that upon returning home my sacrifices for freedom would be recognized. Friends and strangers alike would stop by, I imagined, to express their appreciation, or perhaps even admiration, for my selfless duty abroad. Unlike the confusing, difficult period prior to my active duty service, I would now be coming home to a life of peace and purpose. I was hoping to learn more about leading a religious life, and I was sure that everything else would also fall into place.

Fortunately, we mere mortals are unaware of what the future holds. For had I known the challenges that awaited me back home, I'm afraid I might have lost all hope.

2 December, '69
Quang Tri

Dear Gil,

It's been long since we've talked, and it's very much my fault. I could've written to you ... but I didn't. ...

I can't thank you enough for the beautiful Chanukah present. It's just perfect! I've got it hanging on my wall now, and I'm also mailing 3 postcards (Sept., Oct., and Nov.).[1]

It won't be long now—128 days, to be exact—when I am slated to return to the States. What is the date you will be home? I know you and Deb are planning on a summer wedding ...

How's school going? Are you still as excited about your "learning" as you obviously were when I last saw you? (What a silly question. I really can't imagine you losing enthusiasm for it.)

Let me briefly outline life here, just to give you some flavor for this place. There is so much to tell you, I really don't know where to begin.

First of all, I'm the Signal Equipment Maintenance Officer for a Maintenance Battalion. This means I have the mission of supporting all signal (communications electronics) equipment for all of the units the battalion supports. It's a big job, and perhaps when I return I'll be more at liberty to outline in more detail.

In addition, I'm the Battalion Signal Officer. This means I control (and get chewed out for not controlling) all communications in the battalion. This includes all telephones, radios, radio teletypes, message center, certain computers, and other sophisticated equipment. I really like the job a lot, but if I had the choice between the job and collecting garbage in Waltham, I'd choose the latter before you could bat an eyelash!

Weather-wise, it rains almost constantly here.[2] Many of the "roads" are flooded, washed out, and have three to four foot deep ruts in them. There is only one paved road I know of around here, and that's the main road south to Phu Bai, Da Nang, Long Binh, and Saigon. Everything else is dirt—or more accurately, slush.

I've managed to pick up a smattering of Vietnamese, but not enough to talk politics yet. I can say "Why aren't you working?" though, and I've also learned such handy phrases as, "I pay you big money; you work only a little bit…"

… I'm the Jewish lay leader here in Quang Tri, and we've been lucky enough to get a minion a couple of times now. I also got a Torah (paper) from a friend who's the Jewish chaplain in Korea.

Yesterday the mess sergeant was given a recipe for latkes and tonight I'm writing up an announcement for the Daily Bulletin inviting all Jewish troops to a short Chanukah service each night and some latkes and applesauce. I don't expect much response, however, because many are not as fortunate as I am, and must spend seven days a week in a tank or in an infantry unit along the DMZ or at some other less desirable place.

All for now. Take good care of yourself and please write. I'll try to be a better correspondent.

…

Love,

Your future brother-in-law, Hank

---

[1] Gil had thoughtfully sent me a calendar that had a postcard attached to each month. He instructed me to tear them off and use them to send off a short note each month to his kallah, my sister Debby.

[2] Vietnam's climate is generally hot and humid. Temperatures don't change much through the year. Instead, seasonal variations are marked by a dry and wet period. During the wet season, it rains almost continuously for several months.

CHAPTER EIGHT

NO WELCOME HOME

I learned that I was scheduled to leave Vietnam on March 28, 1970. To my dismay, that day fell on a Shabbos. I was very distraught and did not know what to do.

On that fateful morning, I wrapped my *tallis* around me and *davened* to Hashem for guidance, so that I would make the right decision. I sensed the eyes of the other soldiers upon me, peering out from underneath their covers and wondering about the peculiar prayer shawl their roommate was wearing. (Although I had my *tallis* and *tefillin* with me all along, I had begun using them more frequently during the last months in Vietnam.) I tried putting them all out of my mind; I needed Hashem's help, and the first thing I had to do was pray.

Only several days before, I had heard the sad story of a soldier who had been killed right before completing his tour of duty in Vietnam. He had been serving on a base close to the DMZ and was hit in his hooch by incoming fire on the very day that he was to depart for the United States!

This tragic event shook me to the core, and I realized, more than ever, that my life was in danger each moment that I spent in Vietnam. Thus, I believed that since this was a matter of life and death, I would be permitted to travel on Shabbos and escape a life-threatening situation. (After returning home, I discussed the issue with the Bostoner Rebbe, and he assured me that I had indeed made the right decision.)

I boarded the plane home as scheduled and was soon in the air heading for the United States. The mood on board was festive, and all the soldiers cheered when the plane finally touched down at Fort Lewis, Washington.

At Fort Lewis, I was presented with a Vietnam Service Medal, which is a combat badge asserting that I had served in Vietnam. Then, I stood in countless lines and signed dozens of forms authorizing my leave from active army service. One colonel tried to persuade me to sign up for continued active duty, but I reassured him that I was ready for civilian life. Later, when I recalled my response, I laughed bitterly at my naiveté. How could I possibly have been "ready" for civilian life? I had no clue of what lay in store.

Returning from war to civilian life is always a considerable shock, and one experiences a difficult period of readjustment. After seeing the dead bodies of friends and constantly being in dangerous, life-threatening situations, it is difficult to adapt to everyday life of shopping for groceries, conversing with friends, and worrying about the weather and similar petty matters.

And yet, in a supportive, compassionate environment, a soldier can, to some extent, put traumatic events behind him and learn to function as a contributing member of society. Sadly, though, Vietnam veterans never received this much-needed encouragement upon their return. In fact, the taunts and abuse that we were subjected to, only aggravated our precarious, unstable emotional and psychological state.

This appalling treatment at the hands of our fellow Americans caused irrevocable damage to countless Vietnam veterans. Tragically, many intelligent, promising young men turned into dysfunctional, troubled individuals who had difficulty maintaining long-term employment and family relationships for years to come—and many, for the rest of their lives.

Although I wasn't yet aware of just how hostile the anti-war activists had become, I didn't have to wait long to learn what life back home would be like.

After leaving Fort Lewis, Washington, I decided to stop in Wisconsin on my way back home to my family on the East Coast. A good friend of mine was studying at a university there, and we had arranged to meet on the campus.

My friend was happy to see me and listened intently as I shared my many adventures. Our festive mood didn't last long, though. Other students in the dormitory soon learned who I was and where I was coming from.

"A soldier, eh?" one student remarked scornfully. "So you are one of the murderers who take pleasure in killing innocent civilians."

"What are you talking about?" I asked in bewilderment. "I didn't go to Vietnam to hurt anyone; I put my life on the line to *help* those people. I want them to live in freedom, as we do."

Several more students had now joined the debate, and they all laughed uproariously when they heard my words.

"You really think that we are stupid enough to believe your lies?" one of them spat at me. "The military is only complicating matters there and causing thousands of deaths. The Vietnamese people just want to be left alone. Because of *you* and your friends, they hate all Americans. They can't wait to get rid of you all!"

I tried to answer them and explain that this was not true, but nobody gave me a chance to speak. As soon as I opened my mouth, the other students joined in, until they were all yelling and gesturing wildly at once. Some of them seemed ready to physically assault me and were barely restraining themselves on account of my friend, who was now quite embarrassed to be associated with me.

Although I had been aware of the many student riots all over the nation, I had never come face to face with the peaceniks before. Now, I found myself all alone on hostile territory, surrounded by a rowdy group of people eager to spit on my uniform. I had worn it proudly until that day, but now it suddenly became something to be ashamed of. In the eyes of many of my countrymen, I realized, it marked me as a villain and murderer.

Heartbroken, I decided to cut my visit short. I couldn't get off that campus fast enough. Not only had my joyful reunion gone sour, but I was so overwhelmed by disappointment and hurt that I was physically in pain.

Completely disillusioned, I finally reached my parents' home in Waltham, Massachusetts. Although everyone was overjoyed to see me back alive, here, too, I didn't receive the warm welcome I had envisioned. Like the rest of the nation, my family had been influenced by the anti-war propaganda. Although my siblings tried not to voice their viewpoints in my presence, it was difficult to avoid the topic. After all, the entire country had been swept up by the debates on the war.

Moreover, to my dismay, I learned that my own brother had been arrested in an anti-war demonstration in Washington D. C. *while I had been serving in Vietnam*. I didn't want to be worshipped as some kind of hero, but didn't anyone realize that I had gone there for a cause that I really *believed* in? I had survived several life-threatening situations, and I had been severely traumatized by them. I was haunted each night by gory visions of bloodied body parts and shrill sounds of approaching rocket launchers. And yet, instead of receiving some acknowledgement for my sacrifices and tribulations, everyone just wanted to educate me on the injustice and suffering that the Vietnamese endured as a result of the American military's presence in their country. It was easy to chant "Make love, not war," but these people had no idea what really transpired in Vietnam, because they had been duped by the media and the entire anti-war culture.

The one joyous occasion during that difficult period was Debby's marriage to Gil. The wedding took place only a little more than a month after my return home, on *Lag b'Omer*, May 1970. The Bostoner Rebbe, who had offered Debby much warmth, guidance, and hospitality during her teenage years, served as the *mesadeir Kiddushin*.

After their wedding, the couple remained in the United States until Debby's graduation. Afterwards, they returned to Israel to fulfill their dream of raising a family in the Holy Land.

Back home, as I continued struggling with frightening memories, I became an ill-tempered, cantankerous idler, who hung around the house, grating on everyone's nerves, although I did not realize it then. I was suffering from post-traumatic stress disorder, and my condition only deteriorated each time I heard or read the hateful words of the anti-war activists, who were constantly being quoted by the media and the public at large.

My mother was the one person who went out of her way to try to listen to and empathize with my experiences in Vietnam. She even tried to understand how important religious observance was becoming in my life. One Shabbos, she accompanied me to the Brandeis University chapel. It was not during regular service hours, and I *davened* in the deserted room for an hour or two. As I poured my heart out to Hashem, she waited quietly for me. After my heart-wrenching prayer, we walked home together.

My mother was also a patient listener when I tried explaining to her, as well as to others, why I believed that the United States was doing the right thing.

At this time, the threat of worldwide communist rule was very real. Political leaders of democratic nations believed that the USSR would attempt to influence one country at a time to accept the communists' ideology. Then, once they had the support of nations throughout the world, they would be only a step away from their ultimate goal of world domination.

According to this philosophy, not only did we have a moral obligation to protect innocent civilians from communist oppression, but preventing countries all over the globe from succumbing to communist rule was a matter of democratic survival! The spread of communism in and of itself was a threat to every democratic nation on the map. After all, one only had to look back at recent history to recall how quickly one fanatical dictator with military power could extend his claws of tyranny and cause the death of millions.

Thus, I believed that stopping the growth of communism in its tracks was vital in preventing another reign of terror. It distressed me to see Washington politicians lose sight of their original goals when sending troops to Vietnam. Yielding to the angry demands of anti-war protesters, they were now planning to pull our troops out of that country. The struggles and loss of life endured by thousands of soldiers who had served there would now be for naught. This was no way to fight a war!

Again and again I would express these views to my mother. She tried to see things my way and often agreed with what I said. Still, the situation at home grew increasingly unpleasant when, in addition to my constant irritability, I became more committed to leading a life of Torah. Not only was I difficult to deal with on a regular basis, but now I also refused to eat most of the food in the house and insisted on observing the Shabbos.

With the situation at home steadily deteriorating, I soon found myself following Debby's example, as I began spending more and more time with the Bostoner Rebbe in nearby Brookline. His family was very gracious and invited me to spend Shabbos with them as often as I wished. In addition to helping me in matters related to *Yiddishkeit*, the Bostoner Rebbe, who has great psychological insight, provided much-needed support, as he listened to my struggles and helped me resolve them.

The Bostoner Rebbe's *shul* in Brookline quickly became the one place where I felt truly at ease. There were always young people around my age milling about, and like me, many were newcomers to *Yiddishkeit* and searching for meaning in their lives.

To my surprise, I soon discovered that the *frum* community was the single place where my service in Vietnam was not condemned. There was no name calling or unsettling confrontations. On the contrary, a number of people expressed their admiration and appreciation for my courageous service. Here, I could let down my guard and talk about some of my experiences—although most of the truly traumatic events remained buried deep in my soul, and I was unable to talk about them until approximately thirty years later.

After some time, I realized that it would be wise to move out of my parents' home. The Bostoner Rebbe's son, Rabbi Meyer, was single at the time and lived alone in a small two bedroom apartment several blocks from his father's *shul* in Brookline. He offered to let me move into the flat with him, and I jumped at the opportunity. Since we shared the expense of the apartment, he saved a considerable amount of money each month, and I was finally able to afford to live on my own. It was an ideal arrangement for both of us.

Rabbi Shlomo Margolis, the Rav of the Chai Adam community in nearby Brighton, Massachusetts, was also very influential in my life. Rabbi Margolis was a *litvisher* rav, and I was interested to see what he had to offer. I soon formed a close relationship with him, and he helped me tremendously in my growth in *Yiddishkeit*.

Needless to say, my father was far from pleased when he realized the direction my life was taking. It was enough that Debby had become almost a stranger to the family, and now the son who was supposed to turn into a successful lawyer was about to follow in her footsteps! However, relations between us improved somewhat after I moved to Brookline.

Although my father didn't approve of all the choices I was making, he still tried to be of assistance whenever he could. I had not yet figured out how I wished to support myself, although I did know that, for now, a return to law school was out of the question. Although I knew my Dad loved me, he didn't hide his disapproval of my lack of commitment to finish law school or do something "successful."

I was somewhat of an entrepreneur and began looking into various business ventures. Eventually, I decided to open an import business. When my father learned that I was looking for a business partner, he introduced me to one of his clients, Nathan Towne. Incidentally, he was the person to whom the Bostoner Rebbe later sold his *chometz* before Pesach.

Nate, who was about fifteen or twenty years older than I, made the cash investment, while I put in the sweat equity. My father graciously offered me the use of one of the rooms in his large office in Waltham, so I would not have to worry about rent expenses as I tried getting the business off the ground.

I named the company United Nations Import Export, Inc., because I decided to do business only with countries that were members of the United Nations. At that time, I still thought highly of the organization, believing that it was our best hope for ultimate world peace.

I traveled to Europe to meet possible business associates and attended trade fairs in Denmark, Sweden, and other countries. Eventually, our company became the exclusive distributor of pewter products in the New England area for a manufacturer I met at a convention in Copenhagen. Pewter is a type of metal that is made mostly of tin. It is very pliable and is used to make utensils, vessels, as well as various types of jewelry.

I started marketing the products in the United States and they became very popular. Customers liked the various cups, saucers, pitchers, and trinkets that were available, and retailers eagerly bought whatever I offered once they saw that they sold extremely well.

At last, as I worked to establish my new business, it seemed like my life was getting back on track. I still could not forget about the people of Vietnam, though, and this remained a sore point between me and other members of my family, as well as everyone else I encountered.

One day, my father asked me to join him at a meeting of the Lions' Club, where he was a member. A Vietnam veteran who, unlike me, was *against* the war, was scheduled to speak. My father thought it would be a good idea for me to hear the viewpoint of the other side from a fellow soldier. I agreed to accompany him.

The speaker that night was none other than John Kerry, who had also recently returned from Vietnam. He was just emerging on the political scene as a vocal leader of the antiwar protests and had become one of the organizers of Vietnam Veterans Against the War. Years later, in 1984, he would be elected Senator from Massachusetts, and in 2004, he would become the Democratic candidate who lost the presidential election to President George W. Bush.

There was a nice-sized crowd, and everyone listened intently as he spewed what I believed to be mostly fabrications of his own imagination. He claimed that most Vietnamese people despised the American soldiers and that our men were only causing them trouble. He portrayed random killings of entire villages as if they were the everyday activity of merciless and cold-blooded Americans gone wild. He maliciously maligned his brothers-in-arms and painted a horrible picture of wickedness and betrayal.

While insisting that our presence in that country was wrong, John Kerry did not hesitate to call *himself* a hero. True, every other American in that country was vicious and depraved, but *he* was the one exception. He had accomplished incredible feats of bravery during his time in Vietnam, and he proudly related several anecdotes to prove his courage and gallantry.

My blood boiled as I sat on the edge of my seat and listened to his lies. According to him, my fellow soldiers and I had only been wreaking havoc amongst a people who loathed us. I, on the other hand, remembered the many times our doctors had treated the poor, malnourished villagers and how grateful they had been. I recalled the friendly smiles and greetings I had received during my excursions into the city of Da Nang. Of course, not every American soldier is an upright, righteous person and not every Vietnamese villager was pleased with our presence there, but from the experiences that John Kerry had recounted, it seemed as if he and I had spent our time in Vietnam on two different planets.

As I watched John Kerry speak, I became increasingly distraught. He was a tall, striking fellow and a smooth talker. He exuded an air of confidence and obviously had political potential. In contrast, I was very insecure at the time and not so articulate. I could not stand up publicly and dispute his story. With his self-assured manner and several well-aimed barbs, he would only make a fool out of me.

Still, at the conclusion of his talk, I was so enraged that I could not remain silent. I tried talking to the people who were sitting around me, but no one wanted to listen to what I had to say. They had been so brainwashed by the peaceniks and the media that they only wanted to hear what they had come to hear and believe. That I had been there and had a different story to tell did not matter to anyone.

The only one besides my mother whom I could talk to about my experiences was the Bostoner Rebbe. He was always willing to listen patiently as I recounted some of my horrific experiences and explained, once again, my position. I began spending more and more time with the Bostoner Rebbe, Rabbi Shlomo Margolis, and other people from the Brookline and Brighton communities. As my lifestyle changed, so did my name, and I began introducing myself to people in the community as Zvi, my Hebrew name, instead of Hank.

Without consciously meaning to do so, an ever-expanding rift emerged between me and my old friends and buddies. I was heading towards a new life that they could not possibly comprehend. We were gradually losing common ground and growing increasingly apart.

11 September, 1970

Dear Deb and Gil,

This will be a short one because of the hour – 5 p.m. The sun is rapidly falling, bringing with it some yearned for rest and self-education. Hope your Shabbat will be as relaxing as I intend mine to be.

...

The importing-exporting is coming along slowly, but there are some encouraging signs. (One is the fact that the longer a business stays in business the more chance it has of staying in business! That means that each day UNIMPEX survives its actuarial value increases.) Besides that hunk of massive encouragement, however, is the fact that I put a good 4 to 8 hours into it now each working day. Yesterday, for example, I sent out my first catalogue mailing. 220 publications! Expensive? You bet, but if I get a few good-sized orders out of it I should be on the way to building a MEANINGFUL mailing list.

Gil, how is Yeshiva? Will you be davening on the high holidays for any congregation? Mike Strassfeld will be helping with services at Brandeis, where I'm planning to go.

Health and happiness to both of you and shalom to Kol Yisrael v'kol ha-olam.

Hank

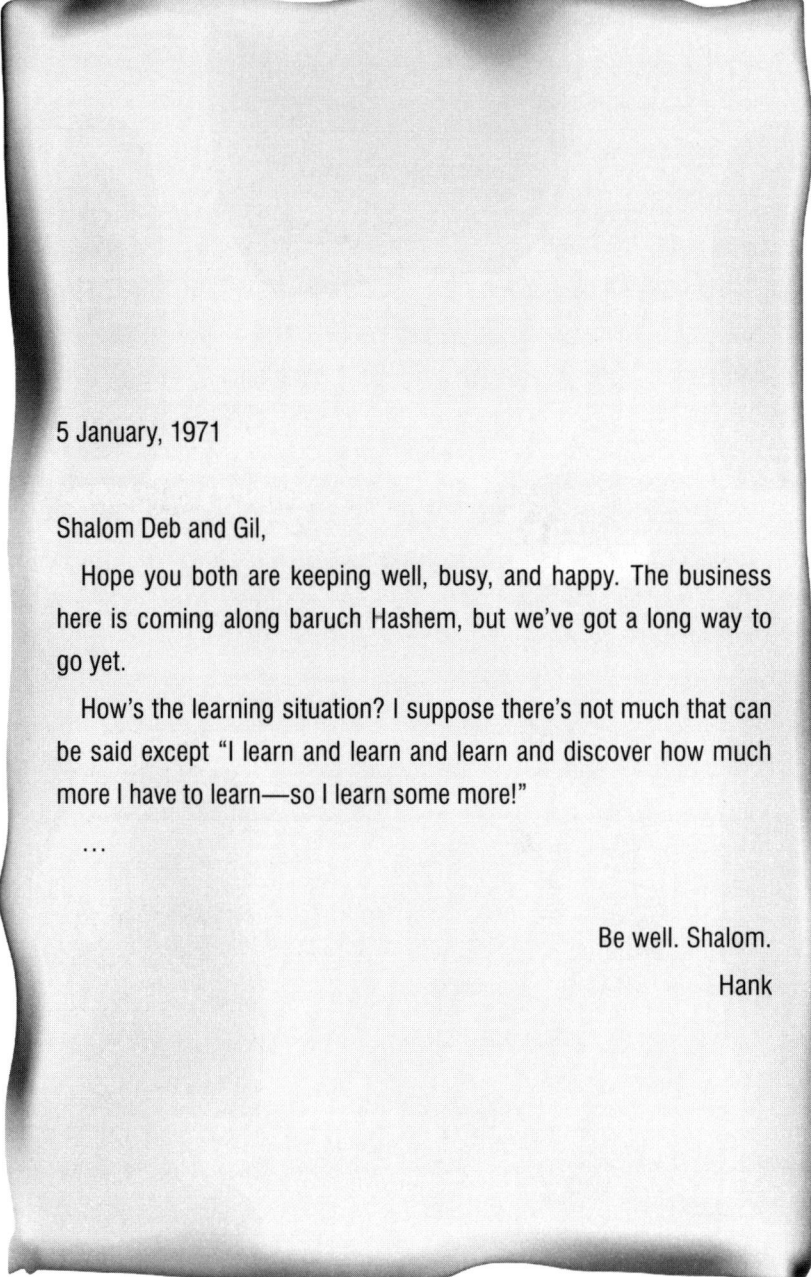

5 January, 1971

Shalom Deb and Gil,

Hope you both are keeping well, busy, and happy. The business here is coming along baruch Hashem, but we've got a long way to go yet.

How's the learning situation? I suppose there's not much that can be said except "I learn and learn and learn and discover how much more I have to learn—so I learn some more!"

...

Be well. Shalom.

Hank

CHAPTER NINE
THE ARMY RESERVES

While I had completed my two years of active duty, I was not yet completely free of my obligation to the army. I still had to complete two more years in the Army Reserves.

While in the Reserves, a soldier spends only several days each month, usually on weekends, training on his or her assigned base. Occasionally, there are training sessions that last a little longer, such as a two-week summer training program. This ensures that all the reservists will be adequately prepared to serve in battle at very short notice. Of course, more often than not, soldiers complete their required duty without incident. However, reservists are always aware of the possibility that their unit will be activated and they will be called to serve.

I began my service in the Army Reserves on June 22, 1970, and I soon found myself spending each Sunday on a base in Boston. In January 1971, I became the Commanding Officer of a Petroleum Supply Company—the 439th Quartermaster Company. If called to duty, my unit would be responsible for supplying fuel to vehicles. Obviously, no war can be fought if the tanks and jeeps are immobile, so fuel is a vital commodity in the field.

There were about 200 men under my command, and each week I led them through the various procedures involved in making sure our unit was ready to perform its mission in the best way possible. Although the atmosphere in the Reserves was a lot more relaxed, we were conscious of our mission to be prepared to travel across the globe at a moment's notice to carry out our assigned duties.

Since I was required to be on base by 0600 hours each Sunday morning, I did not have a chance to *daven shachris* beforehand. Thus, I waited until everyone was accounted for and the morning's activities were under way, and then, at around 0800 hours, I would find a secluded area where I could *daven* undisturbed and put on my *tefillin*. Truthfully, I was still somewhat ashamed of my Jewish observance, especially in this very non-Jewish environment, and I tried to be as inconspicuous as possible. There were some things I couldn't hide, however, such as my *yarmulke* and the fact that I would always "disappear" for an hour or so.

Within a short period of time, my men figured out the reason behind my temporary disappearances each Sunday morning. One day, several guys from the unit approached me with a request.

"Captain Webb," they said, "we know that you are a religious man who understands the importance of prayer. We would appreciate, sir, if you could give *us* time off for religious purposes as well."

"No problem; that's a great idea," I said agreeably. "I'll find a room that you can use, and I'll give you one hour each Sunday for religious services."

The men thanked me for my consideration. "But sir," one of them said, "we also need a priest to lead the service. Can you arrange for a clergyman, too?"

"I'm sorry," I said, "but that I can't give you. I can provide you with the time and place, but the priest is your problem."

After the men left, I was hit by an amazing insight as I reflected on our conversation. The men who served under me, I realized, were lost without a member of the clergy. They required a priest to lead them in prayer. They could not conduct the services by themselves.

We Jews, however, don't have this problem. While rabbis play an important role in our lives, we can speak to our Father in heaven without them. Impromptu *minyanim* have been set up in the most unlikely places, and the people were able to recite their prayers by themselves. And even though a *minyan* of Jews is preferred, we can always communicate with Hashem all on our own from anywhere at any time.

After about six months as a company commander, my superior officer, a lieutenant colonel, called me into his office. He explained that my unit was scheduled to leave for two weeks of training and maneuvers in July. The men would be ordered to appear on our base in Boston on a Friday morning, and it would be my responsibility to transport them down to Fort

Lee, Virginia, where the training would take place. Obviously, this was an important mission, and my execution of it would be carefully monitored and registered in my personal records.

As soon as the colonel explained the operation to me, I realized that I had a problem. The trip from Massachusetts to Virginia was bound to last almost two days, especially considering the fact that we would be traveling with an entire convoy of troops. Since we would depart on Friday, we would still be en route when Shabbos fell at sundown later that day.

I shared my predicament with the colonel, explaining that as a religious Jew, I could not travel on Shabbos. "Sir, I have no problem leading the mission," I said, "but I will be unable to drive on Friday night and on Saturday, due to my religious convictions."

"Look," the colonel said, "my concern is that the men get down to Virginia on schedule. If you can find some way to work it out without driving on your Sabbath, then it's fine with me."

"Well, in that case," I said with a smile, "I'll be happy to do it."

I began making the necessary arrangements, trying to figure out how best to handle the situation. Fort Dix, New Jersey, is the halfway point between Boston and Fort Lee, and I decided that once we reached that base on Friday afternoon, I would turn over command of the unit to my Executive Officer. He would continue the trip with the troops to Virginia, while I would remain in New Jersey with my driver, Private Alan Capone.

Capone was a small fellow, but his name caused some good-natured teasing, as it was the same as the infamous mobster. Capone was a friendly chap, and I got along with him very well. My plan was to give him about $20 right before the *z'man* on Friday afternoon and tell him to have a good time, get a good night's sleep in a local motel, and just make sure to pick me up on Saturday night sober and with a tank full of gas. Then, we would drive all night to Fort Lee, Virginia.

In order to make sure that there would be no snag in my plans, I called Fort Dix about a week before the departure date and asked to speak to the Jewish chaplain. I explained that I was scheduled to make a stopover in the base and asked if there were any religious facilities available.

After a short conversation, it quickly became apparent that things would not quite work out as I had hoped. The chaplain was a Reform rabbi, and he informed me that the standard of kosher food and Sabbath observance would not be up to my expectations.

"I can make one suggestion," the chaplain said helpfully. "There's an Orthodox community just a short distance from the base, in Lakewood, New Jersey. You will probably feel a lot more comfortable there."

I thanked him and promptly called Lakewood. I was put in touch with Rabbi Yehuda Jacobs, who assured me that he would be thrilled to make arrangements for me to spend Shabbos in Lakewood. His warmth over the phone was so genuine that I really looked forward to meeting him.

At last, the big day arrived. It was a sweltering hot day in July, and we were scheduled to leave Boston at 0600 hours on Friday morning. Several of my superior officers were standing around as my men and I prepared for departure. Any problems that came up would be reflected in the ratings I would receive for my performance and execution of the operation.

About two minutes before scheduled departure, I jumped into my jeep, ready to give the "move out" signal at exactly 0600. To my surprise, Private Capone was not behind the wheel. Instead, a six-footer whose nametag identified him as "Specialist Weinstein" was seated in the driver's seat. I had never been less pleased to see a fellow Jew.

"What's going on? Where's my driver Capone?" I asked in dismay.

Weinstein shrugged. "I don't know, sir. I was assigned by the first sergeant to drive you to New Jersey and then to Virginia. I don't know where your regular driver is."

Later, I learned that my first sergeant, who was aware of my special Shabbos arrangements in New Jersey, had arranged the switch. He was simply trying to be helpful when he recruited a Jewish man to drive me there. After all, he figured, if I wanted to do something Jewish in New Jersey, wouldn't I want a Jewish driver to accompany me there? Thus, he thoughtfully accommodated my needs—or so he thought—without consulting me first.

I now had a serious problem on my hands. This Weinstein was obviously not an Orthodox Jew, but I couldn't possibly have my Jewish driver violating the Shabbos in order to accommodate my Shabbos observance. At that moment, though, with all the high-ranking officers standing around anticipating our imminent departure, there was no time to make any changes.

"Okay, Weinstein," I said, "let's move out."

So, out the gate we went with tankers, trucks, generators, and soldiers behind us. Before long we were heading south on the thruway right on schedule. Our convoy was an impressive sight and attracted stares from all the passers-by.

Once everything was under control, I was able to relax and discuss the issue at hand with my substitute driver. I informed him of my plans to spend Shabbos in Lakewood and explained that I had originally intended to allow my driver to spend Saturday however he wished, as long as he made sure to return rested and with a full tank after the *z'man* on Motzei Shabbos.

"But with you," I continued, "it's a different story. Since you're Jewish, I can't have you driving around in my jeep and doing stuff that I myself can't do on the Sabbath. How would you like to be my special guest and join me for Shabbos in Lakewood?"

"Oh no, sir," Weinstein said quickly. "I'm really not into any of that Jewish stuff. I'd much rather just go off and do my own thing."

"Oh, come on," I coaxed. "I'm sure you'll have a really great time. It'll be an eye-opening experience for you."

"No, sir," the man insisted. "I'm really not interested."

"Listen," I said finally, "you actually don't have much choice. I'm a captain. You're an enlisted man. Bottom line is, you're spending Shabbos with me, like it or not!"

My driver was far from pleased, but he realized that he had no other option but to follow orders. Now, in retrospect, as I recall my first Shabbos in Israel, I'm amused at Weinstein's frustration. How ironic that just as I had been subjected to a "Shabbos by force" at the Malon Savoy, I was giving my very unenthusiastic driver the same "no choice" Shabbos treatment.

It was already late in the afternoon when I turned over command of the unit to my Executive Officer in Fort Dix,

New Jersey. I quickly pulled out the directions I was given to Lakewood and read them aloud to my driver. By the time we turned into the Jewish neighborhood, a number of men could already be seen making their way towards the *shul* for *kabbalas* Shabbos.

Obviously, an army jeep with two uniformed men sitting in the front seats was bound to attract attention from the people in the community. Heads turned and eyes opened wide as we sped down the last few blocks. Luckily, we pulled up in the nick of time. Weinstein parked the jeep in front of the Jacobs' home, and I rushed inside to announce our arrival to our hosts.

We were graciously welcomed into the house, and as Mrs. Jacobs cheerfully served us cake and cookies, one might have thought that she routinely served food to strange soldiers minutes before the *z'man*. After we'd had a quick bite, we were directed to a small apartment nearby that had been made available to us for Shabbos. A couple was spending Shabbos out of town and had graciously offered us their apartment.

There was no time to change, so after throwing our suitcases onto the beds, we both rushed outside. I hurried towards the *shul*, with the unenthusiastic Weinstein following several paces behind me. There was no way for two uniformed men to make a discreet late entrance, and once again, all eyes were upon us as we quickly sat down in the back of the room.

The people in Lakewood were very warm and hospitable, and as soon as the *davening* was over, many of them came over to welcome us to their community. Several men inquired about our accommodations to make sure that we were not in need of a place to eat or sleep.

Rabbi Jacobs had arranged for us to eat the daytime Shabbos meal with Rabbi Moshe Rubinstein and his family. By a strange twist of fate, he became my neighbor eighteen years later, when I moved with my family to Monsey, New York, where he is now the Rosh Hakollel of the Lakewood Kollel in Monsey.

Rabbi Rubinstein is a *talmid chacham* of note and a warm, engaging man. He kept us entertained with anecdotes and Torah thoughts as we walked to his home after *davening* the following morning. After inquiring about my background, he smiled when he heard about my years in law school.

"That's interesting," he said, "I also studied law."

"Really?" I asked in surprise. "So do you practice law?"

"Well, actually not," he replied. "I'm not really interested in running a law practice."

"Then why did you put in all that effort to earn your degree?" I asked, perplexed.

He gave a little laugh. *"Kibud aim,"* he said simply. "My mother wanted me to be a lawyer, so I went to law school."

By now, we had reached Rabbi Rubinstein's home. The three of us stepped into the house, where we were greeted by a group of bright-eyed, grinning children. Weinstein's jaw dropped in surprise at the sight of them, and he turned to me with his brows raised in question. I assumed that he was not used to seeing so many children living in one house, and he must have wondered whether Rabbi Rubinstein had mistakenly led us to the local kindergarten.

Rabbi Rubinstein ushered us into the dining room, and we all took our places around the Shabbos table. During the meal, Weinstein and I listened incredulously as the older children recited *parshah* lessons that they had learned. I was amazed at how much Torah they knew! Here I was, struggling to make up for all the lost years of learning, and these children seemed to have mastered it all! I was enraptured by their sweet voices and depth of understanding, and I could see that Weinstein was equally impressed.

During the *seudah*, Rabbi Rubinstein inquired about my service in Vietnam. "Believe me," I told him, "my deployment to Vietnam is the best thing that ever happened to me. Things are very different when you're constantly living 'on the edge' in a war zone. It made me think about the purpose of life as I never had before."

After the *seudah* we returned to our room and were able to take a Shabbos nap. Later that afternoon, when I went back to *shul*, I was introduced to an old man in a wheelchair, R' Meyer Feist. The man had a radiant face and an aura around him, and I felt that I was in the presence of greatness. As I shook his hand, he gave me a friendly smile and warm greeting. I had been told that Rabbi Feist was an invalid who had grown up in a traditional German home and later became a *baal teshuvah*. It was obvious that he was no ordinary man, and everyone in the *shul* honored and respected him.

After Shabbos, Weinstein called his wife on the telephone. Since the apartment was so small, I couldn't help overhearing his part of the conversation. He was trying to explain to her that he had spent the weekend in a *yeshivah* in New Jersey, and not surprisingly, she was having a hard time comprehending it all. After all, wives don't usually expect their husbands to have a religious experience when they go off on army duty!

"Yeah, it's a community in Lakewood, New Jersey," I heard him say. "Near the Fort Dix base. These Jewish guys are really nice. I went to prayer services, and everyone invited us to eat dinner at their home. I really had a great time!"

He told her about some of the people we had encountered, and then, just before putting down the phone, he said, "By the way, remember when we first got married you mentioned that you would like to light candles on Friday night? Well, I really think it's a great idea! Let's do that, okay?"

I smiled to myself in amusement, pleased that another Jew had been positively influenced by a "Shabbos by force." After Weinstein put down the phone, he grabbed the keys and the two of us headed outside. Several *bochurim* and young men we had met in *shul* were waiting for us in front of the house. They all wanted a ride in our army jeep, and we had promised to drive them around the neighborhood before we left.

We spent about a half hour driving around the block with excited passengers in the back seat. Having had such a wonderful time in the community, I was glad for the opportunity to give these boys a good time before heading out.

At last, we could no longer delay our departure. Weinstein and I quickly put our stuff together, thanked our kind hosts, and drove off. We spent the entire night on the road and arrived early the next morning in Fort Lee, Virginia.

After catching up on my sleep, I went out to meet my men, who had arrived the day before. I resumed command of the unit, and after making sure that everything was in order, we began our scheduled training exercises. The days soon turned into a predictable routine, as we spent the next two weeks doing various drills in the field with professional army instructors.

Before long, word got out that there was a Jewish captain in the area who prayed several times each day and observed the Shabbos. After all, a religious Jewish officer is a rare sight in the army!

One day, when I was out in the field with my men, I received a message that a Jewish chaplain wanted to visit me. Although I had not expected anyone to come looking for me in Virginia, I welcomed the visit. It seems that the chaplain had heard about me and had decided to come and see for himself the visiting religious captain.

When the chaplain arrived, I greeted him with a military salute, and the two of us spent some time together. When he finally got up to leave, he let me know that if there was anything I needed, I shouldn't hesitate to ask for his help.

The rest of my stay passed without incident. Before it was time to head back home, I again contacted Rabbi Yehuda Jacobs and arranged to spend another Shabbos in Lakewood.

We left Fort Lee on Friday, July 23. Having just spent two exhausting weeks of war games and grueling exercises in the field, the men were all in high spirits as we got back on the road.

Personally, I thought that the entire expedition had been simply phenomenal. My men had successfully completed all the maneuvers that were required to the general satisfaction of my superiors, and in exchange, I got to spend two unforgettable Shabbosim in Lakewood. Clearly, everyone was happy, and I couldn't help wondering who had gotten the better part of the deal.

UNITED NATIONS IMPORT – EXPORT COMPANY
397 Moody Street • Waltham, Massachusetts • Boston Postal Zone 54
TRADING EXCLUSIVELY IN UNITED NATIONS MEMBERS' PRODUCTS

14 April, 1971

Rebbe and Rebitzen Horowitz and family
1710 Beacon Street
Brookline, Massachusetts

Dear Folks,

Several times I have intended to write "thank you notes" to you when you have shared your home and Torah way of life with me. Each time, however, I somehow sensed that such notes were neither expected nor desired, and that your real pleasure was derived from being on the giving end as much as possible. This impression plus the usual procrastination of the human condition has resulted in this letter being written now instead of months ago.

I want you all to know that especially this week, when there seems to be a particularly great sense of beauty and rightness in keeping a kosher Pesach, your helping me do it is very much appreciated.

Im Yertzah Hashem, the day will soon come when many more children of Israel will sense this beauty and rightness of Torah living and come to it. I hope that whatever influence I may have on those Nshomas with whom I come in contact that the values, attitudes, and experiences which you so willingly share with all who want to search them out, will somehow be transmitted in a positive way to those I touch through life. You are fanning a pleasant fire within me so that I must compel myself to learn and understand more… and discover where it leads.

Chag Sameach. Todah Raba for everything.

Shalom, Hank

CHAPTER TEN
A NEW LIFE

*M*y service in the Army Reserves ended on June 27, 1972. I was finally a civilian again and able to devote all my attention to expanding my new business.

I put many hours into promoting my company, United Nations Import Export, Inc., and worked hard to build up my clientele. One day, as I was walking toward a gift store with my suitcase full of samples, I suddenly asked myself: Is this what I want to do with my life? Work hard and make money? And then what? Life still seemed quite empty. I was over thirty years old, and I knew it was time to find my *bashert* and build a home together.

By now, I had been exposed to much more *Yiddishkeit* than I had in my formative years, and at this point I made the decision that, without any doubt, an observant life was the only one I wanted. I was determined to find a girl who shared Torah true values and would raise a family accordingly.

I began studying more intensely in the Brookline-Brighton community, exploring different approaches to Judaism, such as Litvish, Chassidish, Young Israel, etc.

Most prominent among the great people who influenced me were Rabbi Shlomo Margolis, then rabbi of Congregation Chai Adam in Brighton, and now of B'nai Brak, Israel, and the Bostoner Rebbe, who had a thriving following of both young and old, searching and thirsting for *Yiddishkeit* in their lives.

Although I was not fully aware of it at the time, some Lubavitcher chassidim were also having a very positive influence on me. I liked their genuine *varemkeit*, heartfelt *nigunim*, and welcoming atmosphere, particularly at the *shul* hosted by the Krinsky family.

During the early months of 1974, I met my wife, Chaya Niedelman (then known to her friends as Ilene), through the traditional *shidduch* system. We will always be indebted to Rabbi Simcha and Mrs. Chana Schuck who introduced us and acted as excellent sounding boards as our relationship progressed. Rabbi Simcha's parents, Rabbi Alexander and Rebbetzin Clara Schuck, o"h, were also instrumental in the *shidduch*. We were married in December of that year, and together, we began to build our Jewish home.

Chaya and I lived in Brookline for about one year before relocating to the Jewish community in West Hartford, Connecticut, to be close to where I was employed. By then, I had sold my business to my partner, Nate Towne, and had begun working as a plant manager for a kosher chicken slaughterhouse in Willimantic, Connecticut. This was a new venture spearheaded by my Lubavitcher friends, Rabbis Pinny and Yossi Krinsky. The job didn't last long, though, and I eventually entered the life and health insurance business. My wife and I made many friends in the community and grew by leaps and bounds spiritually.

A year after we moved to West Hartford, Rabbi Yoska (Yoseph) Gopin, an emissary of the Lubavitcher Rebbe, and his family moved into a house a few blocks away from us and opened a Chabad House. Perhaps it was my imagination, but I had the feeling that the Rebbe had sent the Gopins to West Hartford especially to help us in our quest for the path best suited to us. Rabbi Gopin is one of the most caring and energetic people I have ever met, and he had a tremendous influence on me, helping me grow in Torah and encouraging me to explore the world of *chassidus*.

Lubavitch and the Rebbe continued to become ever more important in our lives. Lubavitch seemed to offer a path of growth in *Yiddishkeit* that was very appealing. In fact, it was enjoyable. I attended more and more *farbrengens*[1], both via long distance hook-ups—where we would sit in someone's home and watch the Rebbe *farbreng* on cable television—and also by going to Crown Heights with Rabbi Gopin and others to actually sit with the Rebbe and thousands of other Jews for hours at 770[2].

The Rebbe welcomed each Yid with open arms and a warm smile, and I immediately felt at home.

[1] Chassidic get-togethers where Torah and self-improvement topics are discussed in a non-judgmental and non-threatening manner.

[2] 770 Eastern Parkway, Crown Heights, New York, where the world headquarters for Lubavitch is located.

At a time when most *frum* Jews felt that it was important to focus on strengthening their own communities, the Rebbe worked tirelessly to bring Yiddishkeit to every corner of the globe. He dispatched hundreds of his *chassidim* to places many *frum* people hadn't even heard about. These *shluchim* immediately set to work searching out the Jews, many of whom chose to keep a low profile with regard to their Jewish identity. Jewish people began to feel good about being Jewish, and amidst this newfound interest, the *shluchim* built *shuls*, schools, and *mikvaos*, organized children's rallies, and took to the streets to offer people the opportunity to do a *mitzvah* they may never have had a chance to do before.

The Rebbe referred to every Jew as a "lamplighter." Every Jew must ignite the flame of another Jew. Every Jew can teach. "If someone only knows *aleph*," the Rebbe said, "then let him teach *aleph*."

My growing attachment to the Rebbe was also built on the fact that I had begun writing to him about some pressing personal issues. His responses and advice were always right on target.

One example of the Rebbe's deep insight occurred in the course of our various correspondence. For many years, my exact Hebrew name, Zvi Eli, was the subject of discussion and controversy with the various *rabbonim* with whom I had contact. Was Eli spelled with an *aleph* or *ayin* and what exactly was the name?

I signed my letters to the Rebbe as Zvi Eli in Hebrew, and he responded by addressing me as Zvi Eli' (the abbreviation for Eliyahu). I began using this as my Hebrew name. Some time later, my mother was cleaning out some old papers and found my original Bris certificate. The *mohel* had written my name in Hebrew: Zvi Eliyahu!

These were soul-searching times, but the Rebbe and his chassidim had the tools to teach and the *ahavas Yisroel* to reach out to everyone on his or her level.

Although I had already been *frum* for several years by now, I was still very self-conscious when wearing my *yarmulke* in public. I became even more aware of my head-covering when, after choosing a career as an insurance salesman, I realized that it would probably be a hindrance when dealing with certain potential customers. I would be approaching complete strangers on a daily basis, and without a doubt, many of them would be forming their opinion of me based on my appearance. Furthermore, since I didn't shake hands with women, I knew I might offend a client just as I was trying to build her trust and begin a business relationship.

Indeed, my worst fears were soon realized. One day, I walked into an office hoping to interest a business owner in saving money on group health insurance. The man I approached was so bothered by my *yarmulke,* that he became visibly upset the moment his eyes fell upon it.

"Why are you wearing that on your head?" he angrily challenged. "Do you think you are better than the rest of us? I'm also a Jew, and I also believe in G-d, but I don't wear my religion on my sleeve like that!"

I opened my mouth to respond, but he cut me short. "Look, I'm not interested in doing business with you," he said curtly. "Whatever you have to sell, I'm not interested."

The man was so hostile that I didn't even try to reason with him. I was deeply disturbed by his outburst and I barely managed to keep my head up as I walked out the door. When I was finally out on the street again, I had to take some time to collect myself before I was able to continue with my planned route.

To my surprise, though, I soon discovered that my *yarmulke* could actually elicit a favorable response, as well. In another business office, the non-Jewish owner wanted to do business with me *because*, not in spite, of my head covering.

"I see that you are a religious man," he said amiably, "so I know that I can trust you. You won't give me a bad deal or try to rip me off. Let me hear what you can offer me."

When I walked out some time later, I had opened a nice group case and had some new pride in wearing my religious articles for all to see.

As I worked to build up my customer base in the insurance line, I encountered many different people. Being very sociable, I always take the time to chat with my customers, and this has led to many more interesting experiences.

An amusing event occurred when I had an appointment with some wealthy businessmen in Maine. One of my clients was in the process of buying a business. When I met the seller, I asked, "What are you going to do with all the money from this sale?"

"I'm planning to retire," he explained. "but I hope to spend some of my time lobster fishing. I really enjoy doing that."

His eyes then focused on my *tzitzis*. "What are those strings hanging down for?"

"Oh, these are *tzitzis*," I replied.

"Sitsis? They look like lobster strings to me!"

I then proceeded to explain that wearing *tzitzis* is one of G-d's commandments for Jewish men, and that the purpose is to remind us to do all of G-d commandments.

"Hmmm," he said with interest. "Well, do they work?"

I thought for a moment and then said that one of G-d's 613 commandments is to be honest in business. "They're reminding me about that right now," I remarked with a smile, "so I guess they do work."

He was quite impressed and our business discussion went quite well after that. The experience taught me a very important lesson: If I go in proud of who I am and what I represent, there is a very good chance that I will be accepted that way.

Many years later, I had another eye opening experience. I ran an advertising campaign for term life insurance. A wealthy individual with a strong and unmistakable Southern accent responded and became my client. We had many friendly conversations on the phone on a wide variety of subjects. However, religion was not one of them.

One time, he called before Shavuos and asked me to personally deliver his $2 million life insurance policy. We had already worked out the details and he was prepared to pay the annual premium, but he just wanted to see with whom he was doing business. I agreed to fly out and personally deliver it to him.

"How 'bout Saturday?" he suggested.

"No, I'm not available then," I said.

"What about Tuesday?"

"I'm afraid Tuesday won't work for me either," I said. "It's a holiday."

"A holiday?! What holiday?"

"Shavuos. It's a Jewish holiday," I explained, "and I don't work that day."

There was an audible intake of breath and a pregnant pause. Then in his most pronounced Southern accent yet, he said, "Yo mean I 'bin doin' business with Jews all this time?"

"You betcha," I replied, "and proud of it, too!"

There was another prolonged silence. "Well, when *can* you come out here?" he asked finally.

We set up the appointment for after Shavuos, despite his apparent distaste for my Jewishness. When he asked how he would recognize me, I assured him that that would be easy. "Black hat and a grey beard."

He met me with his white stretch limousine, which was equipped with an amazing sound system playing country and western music. We did complete the deal, but he did not continue doing business with me after that. I, however, still get a little pleasure out of keeping him on our mailing list all these years. He has never requested to be removed.

• • •

After twelve years in West Hartford, with our oldest daughter, Rochel Bina, about to enter the seventh grade, we felt we either had to send her away to further her education or move the family to a community where more schooling options were available.

We began exploring places like Monsey, New York and Baltimore, Maryland, and we decided to write to the Rebbe for advice and blessing. It was about this time (February 1988) that the Rebbetzin passed away, and the Rebbe made it known that he would not be answering every letter that he received. If someone did not receive a reply to a question, he or she was advised to consult three close friends, and if all gave the same response, one could assume that he had the Rebbe's blessing as well.

We wrote to the Rebbe and explained our dilemma, outlining the various pros and cons of the alternative solutions we envisioned. I also mentioned that Rabbi Dovid Wichnin, with whom I had become acquainted in Boston, lived in Monsey now, and I was hoping to reconnect with him if we moved there.

I mailed the letter, but after a considerable amount of time, there was still no response. We wrote again; we faxed letters to the Rebbe's office; we phoned. Still, there was no answer.

After waiting some more, I finally asked the opinion of several close friends, and they all thought that moving to Monsey made the most sense. It was just so prohibitively expensive! Nonetheless, we began looking more seriously at real estate there and actually made an offer on one house.

Despite the fact that we could rely on the assumption that we had the Rebbe's *berachah*—since three friends had recommended the move—I wanted a written *berachah* from the Rebbe. I told the real estate agent, Mr. Waxman, that our offer was to be contingent on receiving the Rebbe's blessing. Surprisingly, he agreed, and we wrote that stipulation into the offering binder. The offer was accepted and we ordered an engineer's inspection report.

Meanwhile, my mother-in-law became quite ill, and my wife began making trips to Bridgeport, Connecticut almost daily to care for her. At the same time, she also had to stretch her time and energy to care for our young family. With so much going on, we felt that it was more important for her to devote her energy to helping her mother than to the concerns of moving.

We called Mr. Waxman and explained that we would have to withdraw our offer, due to various personal issues that had come up, and also because we had still not received the Rebbe's official blessing, as agreed.

Several months later, during Chol Hamoed Pesach, my wife went out to the mailbox and found a letter from the Rebbe. With barely contained excitement, we opened it and read (approximate content, since I have not located the original letter): "In response to your letter dated… (the date of our first detailed letter), M'*shana makom m'shana mazal l'tova u l'brachah b'gashmius u v'ruchnius* (Change your place and you change your fortune for the good, and with blessing, both materially and spiritually)."

We showed the letter to the Gopins and they agreed that the message was clear. "The Rebbe is telling you to move to Monsey!"

Within hours after reading the letter, our phone rang. "Hello, Mrs. Webb. This is Mr. Waxman from Monsey. I was just wondering if you are still interested in that house… "

Chaya contacted me, as I was out of the house then, and we decided to call him right back. "Well," I exclaimed, "would you believe that we just received the Rebbe's *berachah* **today**?! And now you called right afterwards! We are definitely interested, but after we made the first offer, we received the engineer's report, and it seems that there is a significant amount of work that must be done on the house. Considering the cost of these repairs, we can only afford to make an offer that is substantially less than our original one."

Mr. Waxman said that he did not know whether the sellers would accept the lower offer, but he was willing to present it anyway. Later that same day we heard that the seller had, indeed, accepted our offer. Apparently, by now their house had been on the market for some time and they were eager to sell.

But that was only the beginning. We now had to sell our three-family home in order to have the cash needed to buy in Monsey. As soon as we put the house on the market, a young man came over on Shabbos and wanted to make an offer. We explained that we were unable to do business on Shabbos, so he would have to return after Shabbos to discuss it.

He did indeed come back after Shabbos, and he made a substantial offer—five times more than we had paid for the house! We immediately accepted and were now financially able to move to Monsey. I later learned that the buyer suffered a huge financial loss when the current owner bought it through a foreclosure, after the real estate market in that area took an unexpected plunge. Thus, we not only saved a considerable amount of money on the Monsey property by waiting for the Rebbe's *berachah*, but, amazingly, we also ended up selling the West Hartford house at the very top of the market. Talk about market timing! And thank you, Rebbe.

• • •

Indeed, Monsey was the ideal place for us to raise our family. As I had hoped, I did reconnect with Rabbi Dovid

Wichnin, who established the Tzemach Tzeddek Congregation in Monsey, and remained close to him until his passing.

Today, all of our children (except for the youngest, who is not yet married) are establishing their own homes. In another remarkable twist of fate, all of them have decided to dedicate their lives to fulfilling the Rebbe's vision of bringing every Jew closer to his or her heritage. Thus, not only was Lubavitch instrumental in changing my life, but as a result, my own children will *be'ezras Hashem* continue changing many more.

My sister Debby, who is now known to many as Rebbetzin Devorah Eisenbach, still lives in Eretz Yisrael. Ultimately, I was only among the first of many who were so positively influenced by Debby and Gil.

Before my father passed away in *Shvat* of 2000, he proudly expressed his joy in that all his children had married into the faith. Fortunately, he never experienced the anguish of so many of his contemporaries, who watched their children choose non-Jewish spouses. I believe that the Jewish identity that my parents instilled in all of us since our early childhood spared them from this tragedy. Moreover, this heightened awareness of our Jewish identity led Debby, and later me, to further explore our heritage.

Additionally, my siblings and I have not forgotten our parents' admonitions to appreciate and respect each other. It is to their credit that, while other families in our situation have been torn apart by their differences, we have remained a harmonious and loving clan, despite our diverse lifestyles and philosophies. There's Sally—who moved to Britain after her marriage—and her English family; Debby, with her *chassidishe*, Israeli brood; my own Lubavitch household in Monsey; and

Marc, Sam, and Heidi and their families who have remained in our home state of Massachusetts. Nonetheless, distance and life choices have not stopped us from remaining in steady contact, and it continues to be a tremendous source of *nachas* for my mother to watch our camaraderie and affection when we are together.

With the help of *Hakadosh Baruch Hu*, I have finally realized my dream. Frequently, as I sit at the Shabbos table and proudly listen to my children and grandchildren sharing their thoughts on the *parshah*, I remember how I once yearned for just such a family many years ago, when I was a Shabbos guest at the homes of gracious hosts. This day will always have special meaning for me, because, looking back, I realize that it was Shabbos that saved me. First, in Eretz Yisrael, it forced me to come face to face with my heritage; then, in Vietnam, it showed me who my true Commander is; and later, in Lakewood and Brookline, it gave me a dream, a vision, of what I wanted my own family to look like.

Today, my entire week revolves around Shabbos. Each day is a countdown towards the day of the Queen's arrival. Shabbos inspires me and strengthens my faith in Hashem. And every week, it continues to remind me of how far I have come; how fortunate I am to be where I am today; and how much further I would like to grow.

EPILOGUE

A True Soldier Now

By Zvi Webb

Serving in the military was really a great experience, and it taught me a lot about life. Where else can a man in his twenties be entrusted with the welfare of hundreds of soldiers' lives and millions of dollars in buildings, vehicles, weapons, ammunition, radios, and other equipment? Where in civilian life can you find a young CEO who takes charge of a business with hundreds of employees overnight?

That happens all the time in the military. A soldier is trained to do a particular job, and then he or she is thrust into that position. One either sinks or swims. It's real responsibility, and as they say, it makes a man out of you.

Being thrown into the military world with people from all walks of life had an awesome, maturing effect on me. I saw up close how some people can stoop to the lowest levels of living like animals, losing all sense of morality; on the other hand, I saw men who refused to succumb to the laws of the jungle, but rather rose to the heights of heroism, placing their own lives in jeopardy to save others. It was a genuine pleasure and privilege to serve with them.

Some of my experiences, such as the time that I was nearly murdered by a Jew-hating, fellow officer, served as a wake-up call and made me realize that the world is far from perfect. It was no pleasure serving with that bigot, but it did alert me to the need to educate myself much more about my own heritage.

Luckily, most of the people I met in the military were decent men and women. However, whenever I encountered anti-Semitism, I wondered: "Why do they hate me?" I could never understand this unprovoked loathing until years later, when I encountered the Torah rule *"Eisav soneh l'Yaakov."* It's not rational. It's just how Hashem made His world.

After I retired as a captain from the army, I began studying the obligations of a private in the army of Hashem in order to serve my true Commander-in-Chief as a loyal soldier. Although I was now a mere enlisted man—not a captain commanding other soldiers as before— I truly believed that transferring to my new role was the greatest promotion I had ever received!

A private first class is a foot soldier. He's on the frontlines 24/7. That's what it means to be a private in Hashem's army. From the moment one wakes up in the morning until one falls asleep at night, a Jewish "soldier" has marching orders: *Modeh ani, brachos,* learning, praying, giving charity, helping others learn and do more *mitzvos,* etc. The daily mission statement for a foot soldier never ends.

Wanting to be an even more faithful soldier, I eventually became a Lubavitcher *chassid*. In the U.S. Army, there is a unit called Special Forces. Their mission is to go into the most challenging situations, where regular soldiers don't usually go. I viewed Lubavitch as the Special Forces department of Hashem's army. I liked the idea of reaching out to fellow Jews who knew or observed even less than I. As part of the Rebbe's unit, I took part in many fascinating "operations" in various unusual locations. After all, a soldier never knows when he will be called into action!

Several years ago, my wife Chaya and I went to visit two of our sons in Camp Gan Yisroel in the Catskill Mountains. We left camp in the late afternoon and made our way across the mountains to the Adirondacks, where we planned to take a short vacation.

In the Adirondacks, we stopped at a gas station along the highway. A young man, probably in his early twenties, with abundant pink hair was pumping gas into the car in front of ours.

I turned to my wife and said, "See that guy? I'll bet you dollars to donuts he's Jewish."

She was very skeptical, but not one to let a potential opportunity pass by, I said, "Just watch."

I quickly got out of the car and asked him the famous question, "Excuse me, but are you Jewish?"

"Yes," he replied, surprised. "How did you know?"

"Pink hair!" I explained with a broad smile.

After he confirmed that his mother was Jewish, I asked him if he'd like to do something *really* Jewish. He was willing, so I led him to the side of our car, where he allowed me to help him put on *tefillin*. He was also quite receptive to my giving him the name of a *shaliach* near his home.

This experience is repeated untold number of times around the world by other Lubavitcher *chassidim*. In fact, my father actually put on *tefillin* in Brazil, of all places!

My parents were traveling to Brazil, where my mother was scheduled to give lectures in her field. I gave them some money to give to charity on my behalf when they arrived. I also provided them with the name of a *Chabad shaliach* in Brazil where they could give the *tzedakah* and send my regards as well. When my parents called the *shaliach*, he invited them to come over. The *shaliach* welcomed them warmly and persuaded my father to put on *tefillin*. (see picture in photo section)

Sometimes I have the *z'chus* of being pulled into action just because people know I am a Lubavitcher *chassid*.

Once I was called and informed about a severely disabled young man in Monsey with a degenerative disease whose family wanted him to put on *tefillin* daily. They needed someone to fill in on the days that his father was unable to help him. The son was only able to communicate by clicking his tongue or blinking his eyes. I would put the *tefillin* on him, and he would click or blink when he had finished reciting the *Shema* mentally. Although his lips never moved, it was clear that he was praying with much devotion, and it always took some time before he signaled for the *tefillin* to be removed. I was privileged to participate in this *mitzvah* until his passing.

Another time, I was asked to put *tefillin* on a man who had a terminal brain tumor and had requested to do this mitzvah. He was not yet *frum*, but he felt that this would help him. It was a very sad situation, since his two young daughters had already lost their mother shortly before he was diagnosed.

Before he was *niftar*, I was able to help him purchase his own pair of *tefillin*, and he even requested that the food he ate in the hospital be kosher. I hope that I was able to bring a little bit of comfort to him in his last months and some consolation to his family.

Once, when my wife and I were in San Diego with our daughter Rochel and her family, we were on a tour bus when a really scruffy person—the kind one usually tries to avoid—started a conversation with me. He was attracted to me because of my unmistakably Jewish appearance. In the ensuing exchange, he told me that he was born in Germany about fifty years ago to a Jewish mother and German father. That would have put his father in the Nazi, or post-Nazi, era. His siblings considered themselves non-Jews, but he knew that he was Jewish. I had unfortunately left my *tefillin* in my car, and he disappeared before I could get them. That taught me an important lesson. A soldier must always be prepared. (Luckily, I did manage to jot down his name and address, and I later passed the information on to a local *shaliach*.)

Recently, close friends made a *chasunah* out of town, and my wife and I attended. Since this was our vacation time, we toured the city and passed a jewelry store. There was a magnificent diamond necklace in the window that my wife admired, and we were curious to know how much such an exquisite necklace cost. I suggested that we go in and ask to see it.

As soon as we stepped into the store, I informed the salesman that we were merely curious passers-by, and not potential buyers. We did not want him to waste his time thinking that he was about to make an important sale[1].

The man was very accommodating (the necklace was priced at $14,000!), and he was happy to chat with us. He had a decidedly Jewish name, and we began schmoozing a bit about the local Jewish community, whether he had attended Hebrew School, etc. I suggested that I come back a little later to help him put on *tefillin*. He agreed, and as promised, I later returned to the store. He had not worn *tefillin* since his Bar Mitzvah and was very moved by the experience. We spent about forty-five minutes sharing stories, and I was able to connect him with the local *shaliach*.

Every Jew is, of course, an enlisted soldier in Hashem's army by birth. In fact, the Torah actually uses the term *tzivos Hashem*. Tragically, because of the many battles fought by Hashem's "soldiers" in the past century for their physical survival, the spiritual training of many new recruits have all too frequently been sorely neglected. As a result, many of these uneducated troops have "gone AWOL," and thus, as the Rebbe has instructed, I have made it my mission to try to return them to our ranks whenever I stumble upon them.

I try to remain alert to these and all my other duties as a private in the army of Hashem and to fulfill them to the best of my ability. I know we will win each battle and ultimately the war against evil and everything that opposes Hashem's will. I wear my uniform with pride each day, and I hope and pray that both my Creator (our Supreme Commander) and the Rebbe (my unit commander) will always be pleased with my performance.

---

[1] This might be called *geneivas daas*, which is a form of thievery. By misleading others or deceiving them about our true intentions, one is guilty of wasting, or "stealing," their time.

BS"D
Tamuz 5765

Dear Reader,

I'm the serious Gil, with a sense of humor, recalling my first meeting with my dear, illustrious brother-in-law, Zvi (Hank). It was on the Saturday night after his "Shabbos by force" that I went with my fiancée (well, we were almost engaged) to meet Zvi. His relaxed, disarming demeanor was what struck me and I hoped that the rest of my wife-to-be's family would be as nice.

As Hank was always conscious of people and people's rights, he couldn't get over the freedom of the Arabs in and out of Tel Aviv's discotheques. "Where did you see Arabs?" was our amazed comment. "All around," he replied. Now in 1969, few Arabs, if any, deemed the late night party scene of Tel Aviv. "But they were riding in cars and going in and out of restaurants," Zvi said. "Jews don't do that on Shabbos, so they must have been Arabs!" Zvi should have been right. Sad to say, he wasn't.

In the course of our conversation, I invited Zvi to visit me at the Itri Yeshiva, where I was learning. He gladly consented, remarking that he had never been in a yeshivah before and quite looked forward to the experience.

So, on Sunday, at 3:30 p.m., my future brother-in-law walked into the Itri Beis Medrash, on the outskirts of Jerusalem. Get the picture, because it's worth a thousand words. The bright Mediterranean sun was out in full force with nary a cloud in the dark blue sky. Zvi had walked through the beautiful lawn of the Itri campus right through the front door. Unsuspecting, he was hit by the force of 150 students learning Torah. The noise level, although undetectable from the outside, reached high decibel units as Zvi walked in. From his face it was clear that he had expected the silence of a Harvard University library. The din of Torah study forcefully struck him and he stood still for a moment, not knowing what to make of it.

Noticing his sudden bewilderment, I quickly rose from my seat near the back of the Bais Medrash to welcome him. After pleasantries, I took Zvi to where I had been learning to introduce him to my chavrusah (Robert Friedman from Philadelphia) and to make him feel at home. I tried to find an available chair to offer Zvi. Would you believe it?! There was not a single empty chair in the entire Bais Medrash! At 3:30 in the afternoon, the attendance at the learning session was 100%.

Zvi saw my predicament and solved the problem. "I don't need a chair; I'll just stay right here and watch you continue your studies. Please go ahead! Don't let me disturb you."

So I sat down and continued to learn Gemara with my study partner. And Zvi? He slowly crouched over the end of the table to get a 50-yard-line view. The Gemara was coming alive. The myriad letters were moving to and fro, with the backfield in motion. The Rashi and Tosfos were flanking the Gemara, as a deep chord began to resonate from within. As the letters of the text began to move, the pintele Yid, yearning to learn too, was ignited with the fire of Torah. This was a first exposure that was contained for a while. But it nevertheless kept the body warm in the months to come, on alien soil, until allowed to grow into an insatiable Torah conflagration.

As Zvi watched the Gemara from my side, I couldn't but notice from the corner of my eye that he was touched by the Torah of Hashem in a most profound way. V'nasan lanu Toras emes v'chayei olam nata b'socheinu. To a great extent, Zvi's learning of Torah began at that very moment in a Bais Medrash in Jerusalem, on the way to Vietnam.

Gil Eisenbach

BS"D
Tamuz, 5765

Dear Reader,

I'm so happy you read this book about my brother Zvi.

Zvi is a unique person—as sweet as honey, kind, giving, and at the same time, strong, consistent, and determined, striving to be truthful at all times.

I've seen the following scene a few times. We introduce Zvi to someone. The new acquaintance asks Zvi, "What do you do?"

Zvi replies with a smile and one word, "Mitzvos!"

"No, really, I'm serious. What do you do?"

"Mitzvos! Seriously! That's what we try to do." He pauses for a moment. "Ah, you mean for parnassah?" "Yes."

"For parnassah," he explains, "I'm in insurance. That my kli for parnassah."

As much as Zvi is easy-going, he's a stalwart, staunch soldier in Hakadosh Boruch Hu's army—and he's been this way for as long as I can remember, for Hakadosh Boruch Hu's seal is emes and that is really a middah he strives for and defends. Defending truth, fighting for truth, living truth— that's what Zvi is all about. His understanding of the importance of emes has lifted him above the pettiness of this world and enabled him to build so much. Kein yirbeh, v'kein yoseif.

Devorah Eisenbach

APPENDIX I

THE VIETNAM WAR
A brief history

From the 1880's until World War II, Vietnam was governed by France, as part of French Indochina, which also included Cambodia and Laos.

In 1940, Japanese troops invaded and occupied French Indochina. Vietnamese nationalists saw the turmoil of World War II as an opportunity to overthrow French colonial rule and established the Viet Minh, a front organization of the Indochinese Communist Party.

When the Japanese surrendered to the Allies in 1945, Ho Chi Minh, the principal leader of the Viet Minh, used the occasion to declare the independence of Vietnam. The French, however, refused to acknowledge Vietnam's independence and drove the Viet Minh north.

Eventually, the French regained control of the major cities in the south, including Hanoi, Da Nang, and Saigon, while the

Viet Minh controlled the countryside. The struggle between the Viet Minh and French forces continued until 1954, when, after the Battle of Dien Bien Phu, the French public forced their government to reach a peace agreement with the Vietnamese.

France asked other world powers to draw up a plan for their withdrawal from the region and for the future of Vietnam. Diplomats from France, Great Britian, the USSR, the People's Republic of China, and the United States, as well as representatives from Vietnam, Laos, and Cambodia, met in Geneva, Switzerland from May 8 to July 21, 1954, to draft a set of agreements called the Geneva Accords.

The Geneva Accords provided for a cease-fire throughout Vietnam and a temporary partition of the country at the 17th parallel. French troops would withdraw to the south of the dividing line until they could be safely removed from the country, while the Viet Minh forces were to retreat to the north, where Ho Chi Minh would maintain control. Elections were to be held two years later, in July 1956, and Vietnam was to be reunited at that time under the government chosen by popular vote.

This was during the Cold War era, when the foreign policy of the United States was driven by the fear of the spread of Communism. After World War II, communist governments came into power in Eastern European nations that had fallen under the domination of the USSR, and in 1949, communists took control of China. American policymakers believed that if Vietnam would also fall under a communist government, Communism would spread throughout Southeast Asia. This belief was known as the "domino theory."

Thus, the United States supported Ngo Dinh Diem, who was appointed prime minister of the government in South

Vietnam, because of his anti-communist views. Since Ho Chi Minh was favored to win the planned national elections, Diem refused to sign the Geneva Accords. The United States, which acted as an observer, also didn't sign the agreement.

In October 1955, Diem held elections only in South Vietnam and won by a large majority. He then declared South Vietnam to be an independent nation, with himself as president and Saigon as its capital.

In order to prevent Vietnam from falling completely under communist reign, President John F. Kennedy supported Diem's government and his desire to keep South Vietnam an independent nation.

At this time, much of the South Vietnamese countryside were still controlled by communist Viet Minh forces, which Diem soon came to refer to as the Viet Cong. Trying to stifle the opposition, Diem began enforcing extreme, repressive measures. These actions caused Diem to alienate much of the population, and he became an embarrassment to the United States.

In 1963, Diem was killed in a military coup, and the United States hoped that changes in the administration would improve the situation. Additional U.S. advisors were sent to the region, in an effort to keep the fledgling nation from falling under the reign of the communist Viet Cong forces, which were backed by Ho Chi Minh and North Vietnam.

On August 2, 1964, North Vietnamese coastal gunboats fired on the destroyer USS Maddox, which had penetrated North Vietnam's boundaries in the Gulf of Tonkin. President Lyndon B. Johnson ordered more ships to the area, and on August 4, both the Maddox and the USS Turner Joy reported that patrol boats had fired on them. After the incident, the

U.S. Congress passed the Gulf of Tonkin Resolution, which effectively provided war-making power to President Johnson "peace and security" returned to Vietnam. (Subsequent congressional investigations would conclude that the August 4 attack almost certainly had not occurred.)

On February 7 and February 10, 1965, the Viet Cong launched surprise attacks on U.S. bases, killing and wounding American servicemen. President Johnson approved reprisal air strikes against North Vietnam and shortly thereafter, U.S. combat forces were deployed to South Vietnam to protect U.S. air bases. On March 8, the first of these forces, 3,500 U.S. Marines, landed at Da Nang. By the end of April, 56,000 other combat troops had joined them.

At first, the troops' orders were to protect the U.S. air bases, but the mission was quickly escalated to include search-and-destroy patrols in the areas around the bases. By the end of 1965, there were 80,000 troops in Vietnam, and by 1969, a peak of about 543,000 troops would be reached.

In October 1965, shortly after their arrival, the army fought one of the largest battles of the Vietnam War, inflicting serious defeat on North Vietnamese forces. This caused the North Vietnamese and Viet Cong forces to change their tactics. From then on, they would fight at times of their choosing, hitting rapidly, usually by surprise, and then quickly retreating to avoid the impact of American firepower.

The U.S. Military soon realized that the Vietnam War was unlike any other they had ever fought. It was almost impossible to fight small units of Viet Cong fighters hiding out in the dense jungle, and in villages scattered across the countryside; it was difficult to know if innocent-looking farmers were friends or foes. Furthermore, since many Viet Cong fighters frequented the villages, their strongholds couldn't be bombed without causing considerable civilian casualties. Similarly, during retribution bombings in North Vietnam, the civilian population often suffered great losses. While bombers tried to avoid populated areas, the number of raids made civilian casualties inevitable.

These casualties provoked the anger of many Americans, and popular opinion turned against the conflict. Promising an end to the war in Vietnam, Richard Nixon won a narrow victory in the election of 1968. However, President Nixon retained his predecessor's goal of a non-communist South Vietnam, and this could not be ensured without continued war. To keep his promise to the nation, Nixon began bringing home significant number of troops, and he tried to turn the fighting over to the South Vietnamese army.

After several years of further conflict and negotiations, all four parties of the Vietnam conflict—the United States, South Vietnam, the Viet Cong, and North Vietnam—signed the Treaty of Paris on January 27, 1973. The terms provided for the release of all American prisoners of war from North Vietnam, the withdrawal of all U.S. forces from South Vietnam, and a cease-fire between North and South Vietnam.

The last U.S. troops left Vietnam on March 29, 1973. Ultimately, however, the Paris peace treaty did little to end the bloodshed in Vietnam. While the North Vietnamese were ready to put down their arms, southerners refused to give up the fight.

The situation further deteriorated when the U.S. withdrawal resulted in a collapsing economy throughout South Vietnam, as millions of people had come to depend on the money spent by the American troops. While the South Vietnamese army was still twice the size of the communist Viet Cong forces, crumbling morale caused the government to fall apart, as more than 200,000 soldiers deserted in 1974 and returned to their families.

The apparent weakening of South Vietnam led the North Vietnamese government to believe that it could win control over the south and reunite the country through a massive conventional invasion. Preparing itself for a conflict that was expected to last at least two years, North Vietnam launched a massive, final offensive on January 7, 1975. To their surprise, South Vietnam fell rapidly, and by April 30, the South Vietnamese government surrendered and Vietnam was finally unified.

The Vietnamese suffered heavy losses, as approximately 3.2 million of their people were killed. However, problems persisted even after the unification, as widespread hunger and enormous health problems plagued the nation. In addition, the government vigorously pursued communist economic policy, seizing private property, collectivizing plantation, and nationalizing businesses. Mismanagement and corruption became common, and in 1986, Communism was declared a failed experiment and the Vietnamese government began opening itself up to capitalism.

Nearly 58,000 Americans lost their lives in Vietnam, and more than 300,000 U.S. soldiers were wounded, half of them very seriously. Upon returning home, many veterans suffered from Post-Traumatic Stress Disorder, no doubt due, in part, to the hostile environment they encountered at home. The Department of Veterans Affairs estimated that 20,000 Vietnam veterans committed suicide in the war's aftermath. Throughout the 1970's and 1980's, unemployment and rates of prison incarceration for Vietnam veterans, especially those having seen heavy combat, were significantly higher than in the general population.

In 1982, the Vietnam Veterans Memorial was dedicated in Washington, D.C., to commemorate the U.S. personnel who died or were declared missing in action in Vietnam. The memorial, which consists of a V-shaped black granite wall etched with more than 58,000 names, has become a site of pilgrimage for veterans and civilians alike.

APPENDIX II

U.S. Army Ranks

Source: U.S. Army

SECOND LIEUTENANT (2LT)
(Addressed as "Lieutenant")
Typically the entry-level rank for most Commissioned Officers. Leads platoon-size elements consisting of the platoon SGT and two or more squads (16 to 44 Soldiers).

FIRST LIEUTENANT (1LT)
(Addressed as "Lieutenant")
A seasoned lieutenant with 18 to 24 months service. Leads more specialized weapons platoons and indirect fire computation centers. As a senior Lieutenant, they are often selected to be the Executive Officer of a company-sized unit (110 to 140 personnel).

CAPTAIN (CPT)
(Addressed as "Captain")
Commands and controls company-sized units (62 to 190 Soldiers), together with a principal NCO assistant. Instructs skills at service schools and combat training centers and is often a Staff Officer at the battalion level.

MAJOR (MAJ)
(Addressed as "Major")
Serves as primary Staff Officer for brigade and task force command regarding personnel, logistical and operational missions.

LIEUTENANT COLONEL (LTC)
(Addressed as "Lieutenant Colonel" or "Colonel")
Typically commands battalion-sized units (300 to 1,000 Soldiers), with a CSM as principal NCO assistant. May also be selected for brigade and task force Executive Officer.

COLONEL (COL)
(Addressed as "Colonel")
Typically commands brigade-sized units (3,000 to 5,000 Soldiers), with a CSM as principal NCO assistant. Also found as the chief of divisional-level staff agencies.

BRIGADIER GENERAL (BG)
(Addressed as "General")
Serves as Deputy Commander to the commanding general for Army divisions. Assists in overseeing the staff's planning and coordination of a mission.

MAJOR GENERAL (MG)
(Addressed as "General")
Typically commands division-sized units (10,000 to 15,000 Soldiers).

LIEUTENANT GENERAL (LTG)
(Addressed as "General")
Typically commands corps-sized units (20,000 to 45,000 Soldiers).

GENERAL (GEN)
(Addressed as "General")
The senior level of Commissioned Officer typically has over 30 years of experience and service. Commands all operations that fall within their geographical area. The Chief of Staff of the Army is a four-star General.

GENERAL OF THE ARMY (GOA)
This is only used in time of War where the Commanding Officer must be equal or of higher rank than those commanding armies from other nations. The last officers to hold this rank served during and immediately following WWII.

★ ENLISTED ★

PRIVATE (PVT/PV2)
(Addressed as "Private")
Lowest rank: a trainee who's starting Basic Combat Training (BCT). Primary role is to carry out orders issued to them to the best of his/her ability. (PVT does not have an insignia)

PRIVATE FIRST CLASS (PFC)
(Addressed as "Private")
PV2s are promoted to this level after one year—or earlier by request of supervisor. Individual can begin BCT at this level with experience or prior military training. Carries out orders issued to them to the best of his/her ability.

SPECIALIST (SPC)
(Addressed as "Specialist")
Can manage other enlisted Soldiers of lower rank. Has served a minimum of two years and attended a specific training class to earn this promotion. People enlisting with a four year college degree can enter BCT as a Specialist.

CORPORAL (CPL)
(Addressed as "Corporal")
The base of the Non-Commissioned Officer (NCO) ranks, CPLs serve as team leader of the smallest Army units. Like SGTs, they are responsible for individual training, personal appearance and cleanliness of Soldiers.

SERGEANT (SGT)
(Addressed as "Sergeant")
Typically commands a squad (9 to 10 Soldiers). Considered to have the greatest impact on Soldiers because SGTs oversee them in their daily tasks. In short, SGTs set an example and the standard for Privates to look up to, and live up to.

STAFF SERGEANT (SSG)
(Addressed as "Sergeant")
Also commands a squad (9 to 10 Soldiers). Often has one or more SGTs under their leadership. Responsible for developing, maintaining and utilizing the full range of his Soldiers' potential.

SERGEANT FIRST CLASS (SFC)
(Addressed as "Sergeant")
Key assistant and advisor to the platoon leader. Generally has 15 to 18 years of Army experience and puts it to use by making quick, accurate decisions in the best interests of the Soldiers and the country.

MASTER SERGEANT (MSG)
(Addressed as "Master Sergeant")
Principal NCO at the battalion level, and often higher. Not charged with all the leadership responsibilities of a 1SG, but expected to dispatch leadership and other duties with the same professionalism.

FIRST SERGEANT (1SG)
(Addressed as "First Sergeant")
Principal NCO and life-blood of the company: the provider, disciplinarian and wise counselor. Instructs other SGTs, advises the Commander and helps train all enlisted Soldiers. Assists Officers at the company level (62 to 190 Soldiers).

SERGEANT MAJOR (SGM)
(Addressed as "Sergeant Major")
SGMs experience and abilities are equal to that of the CSM, but the sphere of influence regarding leadership is generally limited to those directly under his charge. Assists Officers at the battalion level (300 to 1,000 Soldiers).

COMMAND SERGEANT MAJOR (CSM)
(Addressed as " Command Sergeant Major")
Functioning without supervision, a CSM's counsel is expected to be calm, settled and accurate—with unflagging enthusiasm. Supplies recommendations to the commander and staff, and carries out policies and standards on the performance, training, appearance and conduct of enlisted personnel. Assists Officers at the brigade level (3,000 to 5,000 Soldiers).

Glossary

ahavas Yisroel: love for fellow Jews
aleph beis: Hebrew alphabet
AWOL: absent without leave
baal teshuvah: a penitent returnee to the Jewish way of life
bashert (yiddish): destined
bochur(im): unmarried young men
berachah: blessing
baruch Hashem: blessed is the Name
bayis neeman b'Yisrael: true Jewish home among Israel
be'ezras Hashem: with the help of G-d
Beis Hamikdash: the Holy Temple
chasidei umos haolam: righteous among the nations
chasunah: wedding
chizuk: encouragement
Chumash(im): any of the five books of Moses
churban: destruction, especially of the Holy Temple
daven (yiddish): pray
DMZ: demilitarized zone; the buffer zone between battling armies
farbrengen(s) (yiddish): Chassidic gathering(s)

frum (yiddish): observant
Hakadosh Baruch Hu: the Holy One, blessed be He
halachah: Jewish law
hashgachah/ hashgachah pratis: Divine Providence
Havdalah: ceremony marking the end of Sabbos and holidays
kabbalas Shabbos: Friday night prayer
Kaddish: prayer sanctifying G-d's name said for the deceased
Kiddush: blessing recited over wine before Sabbos and holiday meals
matzah: unleavened bread (eaten on Pesach)
minyan(im): quorum of ten men for prayer service
mitzvah: Torah commandment
mesadeir Kiddushin: one who officiates at the marriage ceremony
M.O.S.: military occupational specialty
m'vatel: surrender, negate
nachas: joy, pleasure
negiah: physical contact
niftar: passed away
nigun(im): song(s)
o"h (olav hashalom): may peace be upon him
R&R: rest and recuperation; rest and relaxation; short vacation from active duty
parshah: portion of the Torah read each Shabbos
seder: Pesach holiday meal
sedrah: portion of the Torah (see *parshah*)
sefer/seforim: (Jewish) book(s)
seudah: meal

sh'tichye: may she live (and be well)

shachris: daily morning prayer

shaliach/ shluchim: lit.: messenger(s); emissary of the Lubavitcher Rebbe

shidduch: matchmaking

shomer Shabbos: Shabbos observer

shul (yiddish): synagogue

siddur: prayer book

smichah: rabbinical ordination

tallis/tallaisim: prayer shawl(s)

talmid chacham: Torah scholar

tefilas haderech: prayer recited during travel

tefillin: phylacteries

tzitzis: fringes; fringed four-cornered garment worn by Jewish men

varemkeit (yiddish): warmth

yarmulke: skullcap

yeshivah: school for Jewish studies

Yiddishkeit (yiddish): Judaism

Yom(im) tov(im): Jewish holiday(s)

z'chus: merit

z'man: lit.: time; exact time for candle lighting or *havdalah,* when the Shabbos or holiday begins or ends